WAKE UP... LIVE THE LIFE YOU LOVE
THE POWER OF TEAM

Little Seed Publishing
Laguna Beach, CA

Pre-Press Management by New Caledonian Press
Text Design: Angie Kimbro

Cover Design and Illustrations: K-Squared Designs, LLC, www.k2ds.com
Publisher intends this material for entertainment and no legal, medical or other professional advice is implied or expressed. If the purchaser cannot abide by this statement, please return the book for a full refund.

Acknowledgement is made for permission to quote copyrighted materials.

Publisher acknowledges that certain chapters were originally published in similar or identical form in other *Wake Up...Live the Life You Love* books and reprinted by permission of Little Seed Publishing, with all rights reserved.

For information, contact Little Seed Publishing's operations office at Global Partnership: P.O. Box 894, Murray, KY 42071 or phone 270-753-5225 (CST).

Distributed by Global Partnership, LLC
608-B Main Street
Murray, KY 42071

Library of Congress Cataloguing In Publication Data
Wake Up...Live the Life You Love: Team
ISBN-10: 1-933063-10-6
ISBN-13: 978-1-933063-10-2

$14.95 USA $14.95 Canada

Other books by Steven E, and Lee Beard

Wake Up...Live the Life You Love:
...First Edition
...Second Edition
...Inspirational How-to Stories
...In Beauty
...Living on Purpose
...Finding Your Life's Passion
...Purpose, Passion, Abundance
...Finding Personal Freedom
...Seizing Your Success
...Giving Gratitude
...On the Enlightened Path
...In Spirit
...Finding Life's Passion
...Stories of Transformation
...A Search for Purpose
...Living in Abundance

WAKE UP...
LIVE THE LIFE YOU LOVE

The Power Of Team

TABLE OF CONTENTS

FOREWORD

How many times have you found yourself struggling with life itself; unable to keep going or baffled about your next step? You can see the end; you can visualize the victory, but you can't get to the goal, no matter how hard you work or what sacrifices you make.

It just doesn't seem fair.

There are so many of us who climb the steep, frustrating, lonely path to success without ever reaching the pinnacle. We plan and strive and dream of happiness without growing one step closer to the most accessible of all human joys. Even if we give it everything we have, there is still only so much we can achieve. We all have our strengths, but we also have weaknesses.

This is one journey where "going alone" isn't always the best solution. Why try to take it all on by yourself? If you surround yourself with others who can help, you can build more than any individual could. Then, and only then, will you be able to reach your full potential. Then, and only then, can we achieve true success.

A group of likeminded individuals can accomplish tasks that none could achieve alone. A group of complementing minds, each with unique skills and talents, can turn the operation of a complex organization into a smooth, dynamic flight rather than the hectic frustration that a lone individual would suffer.

The old cliché warns that there is no "U" in "Team." Well, we might disagree. U can be an integral part of a team. Without a "You" in team, we all go it alone. And we go nowhere.

Embrace your potential–all of "U."

Once you do, then we can get it done.

This collection of essays includes reflections and memoirs; lessons and instructions; caution and encouragement. In the end, we hope that you will find the direction or the inspiration that will lead you to the perfect team. Whether it is a fully functional family or an enterprising business endeavor, the power of team will bring you to your goals with greater speed, satisfaction and enjoyment than ever you could do alone.

Join us in celebrating the power of team.

 Steven E & Lee Beard
Long Beach, California

BELIEVE IN YOURSELF, BELIEVE IN YOUR TEAM
Steven E

Life is always changing. No matter what, it changes. We fall into habits and are afraid of change; afraid of putting trust in others, yet if we believe in ourselves and can rely on those around us, those changes will become a challenge–**an adventure**. You will have the realization that the change IS for the better and you don't have to face it alone.

The next time you come to this door of change know and believe in yourself and your team. You have the choice to create fear or to face the challenge with courage and faith.

Surround yourself with friends who are supportive and positive, who help each other go through changes with a positive outlook. Face those life challenges with a team of encouraging friends who can help you face the difficulties and enhance your enthusiasm. There are times when you have to go it alone, but when you have support you will be stronger, more versatile, and have moral support to fall back on when you hit those rough patches in the road. In many areas of life finding a few capable, reliable people to help, advise and support you can make a world of difference in your ability to achieve and succeed.

You can't win a football game with only one player. The same applies to running a business, a family, and even a recreational group. You need others to fulfill certain roles. In an office you need a secretary, an accountant, employees and a boss. Take out any of those necessary people and your business won't run as smoothly as it could. Hire exceptional people and things will turn out even better. Finding that perfect team–that team you mesh with in an exceptional way–is a sure step on the road to success.

You can do and be whatever you desire in life, if only you believe in yourself and your team and know that together, you can!

 Steven E

SEPARATED TO BE ELEVATED
John Di Lemme

If you are a champion, you will be promoted to higher realms of leadership. Life has a way of elevating true champions. Just as cream rises to the top of milk, true champions rise to the top of companies, projects and great events.

When that happens, old relationships may fall away. It can be emotional and difficult, but that's part of the price of leadership. Champions must be separated from the crowd before they can be elevated to prominence.

I only hang out with champions. My mastermind team consists of wonderful, fired-up success maniacs who strive to succeed in every area of their lives. They support and encourage my "why" in life, and I support them in the same way. But, not one of them is someone I knew in the past. Except for my parents and family members, not one of my friends from my old days is around me today. Think about that—I separated myself from old ways and old places. That's not prideful talk; I'm humbled and grateful for the blessings of God which have elevated me. But, I'm telling you that one price that champions have to pay is being separated from the "old gang."

I won't tell you that this is an easy process, because it isn't. Sometimes it happens naturally when you begin to immerse yourself in positive self-development materials and activities. One day you will look around and see that you are surrounded by positive, like-minded people. Believe me, naysayers don't want to hang around with someone who always speaks empowering words or has a positive outlook on life despite obstacles.

On the other hand, sometimes those friends who are always dragging you down just decide to hang around and try harder to squash your "why" in life. So what do you do? You have to exercise the gift of good-bye. Explain to those people that you are on a path to success and you cannot allow them to steal your dreams. It's like a bad apple in a barrel of delicious red apples: That bad apple becomes cankerous and destroys all of the bright, vibrant apples. This is what happens when you allow those so-called friends to continually badger you with their negative nonsense.

I will admit that I am always ready to embrace goodbye. I only spend time with champions. Of course, I'll help someone who is struggling to find success. I am a mentor and I'm pretty good at spotting a champion in the making. You've seen them, too; they're not addicted to negative attitudes and words. They are always searching the horizon in order to spot the future. When they see it, they go for it. I will always have time to help those people—champions struggling to be born.

It is not hateful to tell someone goodbye—rather, it's faithful. It's faithful to your own dream and to living the life of a champion. It's not a personal thing; you should never be cruel or dismissive of others, but you have to respond to the call of success. That call will always separate you before it elevates you.

I have seen people elevated while trying to hang on to someone from the old days. If they continue, the old buddy will often trip them up— not because he's a bad guy, but because he's addicted to negativity. It's like eagles trying to hang out with pigeons. There's nothing wrong with pigeons, but they will *never* be eagles. You are an eagle! Fly higher than the pigeons and don't look down.

If you're making $50,000 a year, start hanging out with people who make $200,000 a year. Learn their secrets. Ask them to teach you. That's what "separated to be elevated" means. You make a choice about the kind of influences, the kind of people, the kind of books, the kind of movies and the kind of material that you will allow into your mind.

This is serious stuff. If you were determined to become physically fit and healthy, you wouldn't continue to hang out with Twinkies, donuts, beer and Doritos. You would find the gift of goodbye; you would move out of the old nutritional neighborhood. You would allow yourself to be separated from McDonalds and Pizza Hut in order to be elevated to healthy power foods. Suppose you tried to be healthy, but said, "I can't leave my old friends—the fries, the cakes, the milk shakes—I can't forsake them!" How long would your dream of health and physical fitness last?

You have a decision to make. Are you going to be a champion? Are you willing to pay the price? The struggle is vitally important. It does something in you and for you. I've never known a champion who didn't have to struggle with shaking off the old in order to embrace the new. The obstacles you face in life will lay a foundation for massive growth.

Remember: Sometimes between the separated and the elevated there is a very lonely period. You've been separated from your old friends and have not yet integrated with champions. That is a real testing time. I was in my 20s when I made the decision to leave my old friends behind. At that time, I was surrounded by many so-called friends who called me daily to "hang out." It wasn't until I began my journey to success that I finally realized I was wasting precious time by hanging out with that crowd. I wanted so much more out of life and believed I could achieve it. Unfortunately, my friends weren't ready to step out in faith and build new lives for themselves. After a while, I noticed that the phone stopped ringing and I rarely saw any of those people. It was very lonely but I eventually met new friends who believed in me as much as I believed in myself and my "why" in life.

If you want to achieve greatness in your life, then you have to make the decision to develop a mastermind team of positive, influential people who are success-driven and who believe in you. Have you ever tried to steer a parked car? Not much excitement there. It's far better to steer a car that's moving. The power steering is flowing, the tires are moving on the highway, and you can gently and effortlessly glide that vehicle right up onto the road. When you try to steer from a parked, no power, cold-engine spot on the driveway, nothing happens. Success is like that. You will never be able to turn the key in your heart and travel down the road of success without first pulling out of the old, comfortable parking spot of negative associations.

You're a champion! Your car is already moving! The fact that you're reading this article and not a comic book or other time-wasting material means that your car is moving pretty well. Just keep rolling—right on past the slower cars, the older cars and the beat-up pick-ups that have not been maintained. You were destined for higher elevations. It's time to go for it!

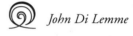 *John Di Lemme*

THE DIFFERENCE A TEAM MAKES
Ryan Carnahan

I was born in Calgary, Alberta, Canada on October 12, 1978. My parents divorced when I was young and it presented some challenges in my life. I think my mom got the tough end of the situation, in that she cared for my sisters and me during the school year. My mom, Beverly, is one of the strongest and most caring people I know. Growing up, I may have had my own opinions about choices made for the family, but today I know that my mom did a terrific job with what she offered me and continues to offer in the form of support in my life. I also believe that it may have been easier for my dad because we spent part of the summer holidays with him, going on camping trips, fishing and doing other outdoor activities. I know that our leaving each year was genuinely hard on him and that he personally believes that he has failed us in many areas.

My mom met my stepfather, Alan Jones, some years after her divorce from my dad. Alan was great at providing time to help with homework, had a great entrepreneurial spirit and a very caring, genuine heart. However, he felt overwhelmed by his shortcomings and his family's humble beginnings and it always presented a barrier to achieving the things he really wanted in life. I am very grateful to have had Alan in my life to provide me with a role model for increasing my tolerance for taking risks.

I loved writing in elementary school, and I had a particular friend, Theresa, with whom I spent many lunch hours writing short stories that we shared with our classmates. I still remember one of the titles, *The Big Adventure*, which centered around two spies who worked together—and happened to have our first names. The more time we spent together, however, the more students teased us, until she did not want to spend time with me anymore. After that, writing became a source of pain, and I did not enjoy the academic writing projects I had to complete in later years of my schooling.

My outlet for acceptance and self-worth in my life was striving toward academic success. I was not a popular kid and excelling in academics felt like an empty pursuit by the time I graduated high school at the top of my class. I spent long hours studying, even foregoing fun with friends. When my father chose not to attend my graduation, I think my entire view of education changed. Even though I did a decent job obtaining my bachelor of science degree in electrical engineering from the local university, I knew that I had lost a lot of interest in what I was doing in life. Looking back on the situation—my father was unemployed at the time—I think his pride prevented him from facing me and the rest of the family. My father inspires me because I want to make different choices in my life so that I do not look back and feel regretful for things that might have been.

But it was a near-fatal car accident in 2001 that finally led to some major changes in my life. In the first few years after the accident, I was introduced to a personal development company by one of my health practitioner offices. T. Harv Eker and his wonderful team at Peak Potentials had a great impact on me. They brought me back to focusing on what I love to do and helped me gain a closer sense of what was great and awesome about me, rather than focusing on what I thought others believed about me.

Having met many people through networking at Peaks events and having gone outside my personal comfort zone, I met two like-minded gentlemen at a charity evening in the summer of 2006. Jeremy Korzeniowski and Stéphane R.J. Bohémier introduced me to the financial services industry, where I had the opportunity to build my own business starting part-time in parallel with my current career. After learning about my own financial situation, I became very passionate about educating consumers about financial products and services that are not traditionally presented in the educational system. It is no wonder people today are in a debt crisis and not making investments that will give them returns that can provide a dignified retirement. In my own family's financial situation, a simple thing like having the right life insurance became a major deal. When my stepfather passed away from cancer in June 2005, his term life insurance paid out to my mom, covering her mortgage and providing some money during the grieving process. If my mom and Alan only had mortgage insurance, potentially, only the house would have been paid off. Good for the bank, but only of limited benefit to my mom. Many third-party financial experts and authors encourage buying personal term insurance and investing the difference, but few insurance companies today separate their life insurance from their investment products. I have seen the impact of this industry in my own family's life and I know I can passionately share the education to empower many families to have the best financial roadmap possible to take care of them right into their retirement years.

Throughout my life, I have had to quit so many business opportunities. I knew it was a fit when I met a team that embodied what I had seen from many happy and successful entrepreneurs: An upbeat, enthusiastic environment where inspiration is the focus and a family-oriented business system is encouraged. I am grateful every day that I met Jeremy and Stéphane, and for the opportunity they have shared with me and the friendship that has resulted. I am also thankful for the fantastic team and friends I work with every day. They provide exceptional coaching, limitless love and inspiration for me to go out and make a difference!

 *Ryan Carnahan*

THE VALUE OF TEAMWORK
James Kwaku Ocansey, Ph.D.

Teamwork occurs when individuals come together to employ their shared resources—minds, energy and hearts—to meet challenges for the purpose of solving a problem. Individuals are limited in what they can do alone. "One is too small a number to achieve greatness," according to Dr. John C. Maxwell. He lays down some principles in his book, *The 17 Indisputable Laws of Teamwork*. They include such ideas as:

- The goal is more important than the role.
- All players have an area to which they add value.
- Winning teams have players that make things happen.
- Vision gives team members direction and confidence.
- Teammates must be able to count on each other when it counts.
- Shared values define the team, and interaction fuels the team.
- The difference between two equally talented teams is the leadership.

How do these principles work? And though each is important, which do we need most to promote and develop our businesses?

Peter Grazier points out that "our needs for sustenance, safety, security, belonging, recognition and a sense of growth and achievement become strong drivers (motivators) of behavior." These are the reasons we perform as we do as individual members of a team. Factors that influence team motivation include:

1. **A clear purpose, focus or mission.** The individual asks if his personal needs and desires align with the mission and focus of the group.
2. **Challenge.** This refers to the level of difficulty faced by the group.
3. **Camaraderie, meaning comradeship, fellowship and loyalty.**

This means that in addition to the technical skills each member brings to the team, there is also the need to relate to one another. There is a need to maintain good interpersonal relationships. The group should work hard to develop and maintain good relationships by recognizing and praising each other's contributions.

4. **Responsibility**. This refers to stimulation generated by having ownership in an identifiable block of work. It also means that the member has the responsibility to bring about change in the group. This includes discipline to bring about positive change for the common good.

5. **Growth**. This includes personal and team growth, which can also sustain long-term motivation. This provides avenues for individuals to learn new concepts, expand their skill bases and stretch their minds.

6. **Leadership**. The best leaders create conditions in which the team motivates itself. The leader also "understands the importance of team purpose, challenge, camaraderie, responsibility and growth, and focuses much of their time on creating the conditions for these to exist." They understand that their team members have needs, and that sustaining motivation and growth requires them to meet these needs.

So how can you incorporate these principles into your own business? What we learn is that the leadership must have a clear vision or mission statement that also addresses personal needs of the individual team members. A mission statement must include ideas that appeal to the individual and with which he can align himself. A good example of this is the Wake Up...Live the Life You Love company. The company identifies itself as a family, and individuals testify to this fact. The company states:

> *The team is made up of experts in the field of writing, editing, marketing, public relations, sales, Web design, career development and professional speaking.*

The company also makes a commitment to the individual that he will be provided "with the resources, support and tools" needed to succeed. This is an excellent example of a clear mission statement or goal that links the individual's personal needs and desires to the overall goal of the Wake Up Team.

The group must also seek effective ways to combine skills with interpersonal relationships. Specific effort must be made to affirm each member of the team by sharing and affirming each person's value through praise and rewards. Opportunities for individual growth within the team enhance the individual's personal growth while simultaneously contributing to the overall effectiveness of the business or team.

Frontline Leadership has suggested nine ways to build your team. These were suggestions given by team leaders who found that these specific practices helped keep up the motivation of the team and so helped to build it. Many multi-level marketing groups that work with large numbers of people exemplify these principles. The suggestions are:

- Playing games together in order to give team members the opportunity to work together.
- Communicate the value that each member brings to the team. This is done by taking time to affirm each team member and share how each is contributing to the success of the team.
- Plan a team retreat. The team needs to come together for a time to plan, dialogue and be refreshed.
- Champion your team to your customers. When you show respect for your people, others will do the same.
- Do community service together, such as serving meals to senior citizens or working as a team with Habitat for Humanity.
- Encourage team members to talk about their families. This helps build a solid bond.
- Explore, understand and appreciate differing work styles. There is need to understand the distinct ways in which everyone on the team works most effectively.

- Learn to laugh together. This encourages team members to let down their respective guards and learn to laugh with each other.
- Delegate authority and provide the resources for your team members to make decisions. When things go right, the credit goes to the team; when things go wrong, the leader assumes responsibility by defending the team's decision.

Finally, the principle of shared values is extremely important. In the case of a business that is held together by Christian principles, the Bible could be the source of shared values that acts as a cohesive force to lift individuals above their personal needs and desires to act in the interest of the group as a whole.

If you motivate the individual members, foster an environment of honest, open communication and focus on a common set of principles and goals, your team will be bound for success.

 *James Kwaku Ocansey, Ph.D.*

YOU CAN'T DO IT ALONE
Gregory Scott Reid

You've probably heard the phrases, "No great deed is accomplished alone," and, "It takes a village to raise a child." You may have even heard the cliché, "T.E.A.M.: Together Everyone Achieves More," a thousand times, but have you ever really stopped to ponder the truth behind such statements?

Let's face it—when it comes to success in anything we do, nothing can be completed without a great deal of support, even for a solo athlete such as a professional tennis player. Sure, they are on the court alone, but they also had many coaches, sponsors and supporters along the way.

I often speak in public and, following a presentation, it's not uncommon for several people to approach me with a reaction to my message. After one of my speeches, someone introduced himself to me as a "self-made" man, and I thought, "What is this guy talking about?"

He had achieved great wealth in his life, and he did it all on his own, he told me, as he puffed out his chest. This person went on to explain that he never sought help from anyone and all he needed in life was his *desire* and *determination* to make it.

Then I asked him, "How many people work with you?"

"None," he said, but he had about 80 people who worked *for* him.

I then asked him to explain who these people were.

He spoke for about 30 minutes, detailing each of his departments, their job tasks and the managers who ran them. As he was unfolding his company "family tree," so to speak, you could almost see the light bulb come on in his head as he realized that he was not doing *anything* alone, but he'd had a huge support group behind him, all along.

Without his staff, he never could have reached his goals. Everyone from the CFO to the delivery truck driver held a key role in the success and/or set-backs of his organization.

A smile lit upon his face, and he said, "I better change my answer; I have about 80 people who work *with* me."

Now let me ask you, how many times have we thought the same thing of ourselves? That we were in control of everything we do? That we created who and what we are?

If it weren't for the village that raised us (our social environment), the education we received and the input given to us by our associates, where would we be?

Remember this: You are a direct reflection of the five people you associate with most, and your lifestyle and income will be the average of those five people. As the famous Charlie "Tremendous" Jones has said, "You are the same today as you will be in five years, except for two things: the people you meet and the books you read."

Given this, wouldn't it make sense to gather the best people and information you can get your hands on and make your team from that? Just as our "self-made" man thought he was the creator of his destiny, he, in fact, was simply a reflection of the great people he had the fortune to surround himself with along the way.

So, who do you have on *your* team?

Best wishes, and whatever you do, keep smilin'.

 *Gregory Scott Reid*

HOW DOLPHINS TAUGHT ME TEAMWORK
Debbie Griffyn

C an you be a team player if you have never experienced teamwork?

I did not learn teamwork from my parents. Like many children, I grew up in a dysfunctional family. My brother and I always knew that we were not wanted. My parents often told me that I was ugly and stupid, despite my straight-A school record. I know that my parents were just taking out the frustrations of their own lives on us, but that didn't soften the pain. Had they been living the life they loved, things would have been different. I will never forget the last words my mother ever spoke to me: "You are more worthless than the dirt in the backyard where the dog uses the bathroom. I never want to see you again as long as I live!"

Feeling like a wounded puppy with its tail tucked between its legs, I gathered the courage to leave my hometown, vowing to break the cycle of abuse. I could have become as angry and bitter as my mother, but I chose the opposite. I knew what it felt like to be battered, to be the victim and the underdog. Eventually, I began to encourage and empower those who have experienced similar pain, in hopes of helping them realize their own worth and to understand the joy and strength that can come from the power of a team.

When I married, my husband was nicer to me than my parents, but he also did not understand the importance of a team. I will never forget the Sunday morning when he barged into the bathroom where I had spent the night on the cold tile floor vomiting so violently and so often that I could barely raise my head. At 8:30 a.m., my husband came in. He did not ask how I was. He did not ask if he could do anything for me. He asked what I was going cook him for breakfast. When people ask me why we divorced, I tell them that my spirit was suffocated. I was still in search of a life that I truly wanted to live, in which I might feel a

unity and a partnership with my own personal "team." I had long
before made the decision to honor the people I encounter and to treat
them as I would like to be treated.

We are all a team in this game of life, and pounding each other down—
by words or actions—only destroys the goodness in us and drags each of
us down into the gutter.

The most amazing spirit of teamwork that I have ever experienced did
not come from a human being. It came from two dolphins. These dolphins had been domesticated—trained to perform tricks and interact
with humans. The first thing I did the morning I was to meet them was
trim my fingernails. I did not want to accidentally scratch one of these
beautiful animals. I realize now that I was exhibiting teamwork and
respect before I ever even met the dolphins. After attending a short class
on dolphin behavior, the time came for me to have my one-on-one time
with the dolphins. I was instructed to swim to the other end of the
lagoon. I floated in the water with my legs straight down and each of
my arms on top of the water stretched out to either side. I had been
taught that two dolphins would swim up from behind me and I was to
grab their dorsal fins. Ideally, this would happen like clockwork and the
three of us would fly through the water with them lifting me along. It
did not work like that, though. I, the intelligent human, was the one
that was failing to do my part correctly.

As a dolphin approached on my right, I reached out and grabbed his fin
perfectly. As the other approached me on the left, I anxiously groped
into the water but repeatedly missed. The dolphin waited for me. The
dolphin on the right waited, too. Knowing this was a team effort and
seeing that I was having trouble, they waited for me to join their team.
Why? The dolphins had been taught that they must work with each
other and with a completely different species to become a team.

If dolphins can master the power of teamwork and offer me this magical
experience, surely humans can learn to work together as a team as well.

I finally reached out and clutched the dorsal fin of the dolphin on my left and the three of us bonded. The experience of gliding on the water was amazing. I can still close my eyes and feel the rush of the salt water pouring over me as my two partners propelled me forward.

Our next adventure was even more incredible. I swam to the far end of the lagoon again, but this time I floated on my stomach with my legs stretched out behind me. My two dolphin friends came up from behind me, each one nestling his nose into the ball of one of my feet. I arched my back to raise myself upward. The dolphins increased their speed and boosted me out of the water like a rocket! I cannot imagine a more incredible example of teamwork.

I don't believe that a "team" must be defined as your family, your church or your co-workers. We can be a team with one another anywhere, any day. We just have to make that choice. Police officers and soldiers exemplify a team attitude in protecting strangers they may never meet. In working with others, not every team player must be present for the power of team to prevail.

I challenge you to see how many people you can make smile today. They must be people you do not know. This could be as simple as remembering and using your waiter's name at a restaurant. It may mean looking your cashier right in the eye and asking how they're doing. Hold the door for someone, or let another driver pull into the lane in front of you. I know I look silly every time I leave the grocery store carrying an array of brightly colored recyclable cloth bags filled with my groceries. But I am not just doing this for me. I am trying to save a tree for you and for your children, whom I may never meet. You and I are a team. When I, as a stranger, approach you in a store parking lot, don't worry—I am going to offer to return your cart to the store, as I am just walking there myself.

The next time you enter an elevator, watch as almost everyone stares at the door. See if you can make someone smile. They will not all accept your smile or return it, and they may even think you are odd, but you may have made them secretly feel special. They may be just like a wounded puppy, weakened by the problems of their day, desperately in need of something gentle to help uplift them.

When we give to one another, we become a team and we accomplish so much more than any of us could possibly accomplish alone.

 *Debbie Griffyn*

ONCE A REBEL, ALWAYS A REBEL
Phil Gilliam

Most people have their own definitions of what it means to be a rebel. Allow me to give you mine: A rebel is an individual who chooses his or her own path and chooses to live the life they love. I am not recommending that we take a teenage approach to rebellion or be defiant for the sake of being defiant. What I am suggesting is to love the life you choose because you *do* have a choice.

As I tell you my story of rebellion, you will see that everyone, including you, has a choice, regardless of your present situation.

I'll spare you the details of my financially burdened childhood. Let me just sum it up by saying that my mother gave birth to me at age 14. Make no mistake, I love my mother and respect her for doing the best she possibly could.

As a teenager, I was so driven to prove that I wouldn't do things like everyone else that I created an adventurous life. I did everything I could to break the rules. I left home when I was 14 and lived with anyone who would have me. My mother's heart was broken. I floated through five different high schools, a couple of which I didn't leave by choice, worked in places I shouldn't have even been in and did all I could to wreck any semblance of what society would call a "normal life." I was so against being normal that I ditched my own high school graduation ceremony—the fact that I actually graduated is a whole other story by itself.

After I felt I had exhausted all my options, I joined the military, hoping to get some stability in my life. But the rebel in me did not stay suppressed for very long. I even found a way to get out of the military commitment early—and legally. Of course, at the time, I thought the reason I wanted out was because I was smarter than everyone and already knew how to do everything, so the military was just holding me back.

I jumped right back into not wanting to hold a real job. I then came up with a brilliant solution to all my problems! I started the first of what would be three miserable failures at running my own business. Don't get me wrong—each of them started amazingly well and made me money. But once again, I chose to do all I could to sabotage my success. I had no problem doing just that, so I decided I needed a career.

I got a job in corporate America, and for five years, I did everything I could to play by the rules. Except for occasionally slipping up and getting myself into trouble, I climbed the corporate ladder and proved that even a rebellious lone wolf could fit in and make himself—by society's standards—an extreme success. You would think that is where the story ends. Oddly enough, that is where the story begins.

It was in those five years that I discovered how—and, more importantly, why—to live the life I love: real happiness!

During that time, I wondered why, even though I was making more money than ever, I found myself becoming stressed more about money than at any other time in my life. I found myself struggling to get out of bed each morning to go to work. I was physically diminished, gaining weight and completely consumed by maintaining the lifestyle I had created. I was constantly worried about how or when my career would end. Worst of all, I found myself trying to fit in with the people I thought could improve or accelerate my career, even when I knew they were wrong. In a nutshell, I had been happier when my life was a complete wreck.

I realized the issue had nothing to do with having a corporate career, the company I worked for or even the people around me. The issue was that I had chosen to suppress who I really was. I thought because I was financially successful that I should be happy, even though I wasn't doing something I cared about. I didn't even know what I cared about. The good news is I gave myself a choice. I made a decision and so can you!

Let me clarify something. If you truly love your job and you get up in the morning thrilled to go to work regardless of your title or where you work, then *love* your job and don't let the people around you make you think there is any reason you shouldn't! That is their burden—let them keep it! Love your work and do it the best you can every day. Live the career life you love!

Neither am I advocating that you quit your job if you're not completely in love with it. I am suggesting that, if you are not satisfied, you take steps to create opportunities that will give you that option if you choose.

The steps are simple:
1. Make a choice. (Doing nothing is making a choice.)
2. Educate yourself. (Not necessarily formal education.)
3. Believe in yourself. (If you don't believe in yourself, get a coach to help you.)

That is exactly what I did, and still do every day! "Easier said than done," you might say. But when you begin to educate yourself, ask these questions: "If I could do anything I wished each day, what would it be?" and, "What problem would I like to solve, and for whom?" (It could be your own!)

Soon you will discover what your passion truly is. Then, either choose to follow it or don't. At least you are allowing yourself to make choices!

Oddly enough, this rebel found his passion in teaching others. I chose to create a company designed to help men interact with women and show them how to have passionate relationships. Because of these contributions I am making to the lives of others—playing a key role in improving the life of the team—I wake up each day thrilled to start working on whatever the day will bring. On top of that, my physical health, mental well-being and my income have improved!

Stop living life feeling trapped and believing that if you take a risk the likely outcome will be failure! The reality is that if you are unhappy or you know there's something bigger and better out there for you professionally or personally, your true failure is in making the choice to stay safe—to do nothing. You don't have to quit your job, start a company or solve world issues! For each of us, the level of risk we take should only be measured by ourselves, not by other people's standards.

I leave it to you to decide. I am certain that you are capable of making the perfect decision for you to release that powerful rebel within you and share your gifts! But be prepared, because if you do make that choice, you could find yourself living the life you deserve and wake up one morning to find you are living the life you love!

Are you ready?

 *Phil Gilliam*

THE POWER OF RESTROOM NETWORKING
Maria Ngo and Ray DuGray

Have you ever reflected on your success and reminisced about how you arrived where you are today? Did you recognize that there were key individuals or organizations that helped you during your success journey?

Maybe an individual said a simple encouraging word; believed in you. Perhaps someone referred you, and that person became an important and lucrative client. Or possibly it was meeting a future business partner in the men's restroom during a conference. You never know what or where opportunities will arise. It just so happens the men's restroom was where a business friendship began for us.

We received an e-mail from Tom Antion inviting us to a *Maximizing Success Wealth Building* event in Scottsdale, Arizona. Despite our busy schedules, we made the decision to attend the event. Our objective was to make contact with some of the very impressive speakers at the event and arrange personal interviews as part of our doctoral research studies in entrepreneurship. We were also seeking networking opportunities with subject matter experts for our upcoming Success Mastery event. The conference exceeded our expectations.

Maria's story:
At the event, Ray, my husband and business partner, approached me as I was sitting in a presentation and handed me a business card without saying a word. The card read, "Authors Wanted! *Wake Up...Live the Life You Love* book series" and the contact name was Lee Beard. I wasn't sure what Ray had in mind.

I was pulled out of the session and led down the hallway toward a gentleman. Ray introduced me to Lee Beard and informed me we were meeting with him and his wife, Linda, for lunch. I still had no clue why we were meeting with him or who he was. At lunch, while we waited for the Beards to arrive, Ray began to explain how he met Lee in the men's restroom where Lee inquired about our business. I found this hilarious! Oh, the images that ran through my mind. Networking in the restroom—what a concept! Before Ray could go on, the couple arrived. At one point during our meeting, Lee turned to me and asked me for more information on our projects. I looked in his eyes and said, "I have no idea why we are meeting." He laughed, understanding that Ray did not have the chance to fill me in.

As it turned out, Lee and Steven E from *Wake Up...Live the Life You Love* had a network of authors, speakers, trainers, entrepreneurs and business owners who would be ideal for our interviews and also for our network as subject matter experts. This was a match.

Ray's Story:
I felt sorry for Maria during our meeting. Everything happened so fast that I didn't have a chance to brief her (no pun intended) about our restroom meeting. I took over following Lee's inquiries to allow Maria to connect the dots.

Lee wanted to know who we were and what we did. I responded, "We are the 'Entrepreneur Doctors.'"

Lee picked up instantly on the branding strategy and meaning behind the title. He clarified, "Entrepreneurs tell you what hurts in their business, and you lead them to resources that can fix their ailments."

Exactly! So, now our new slogan is "Tell us where it hurts." From there, the conversation led to our proposed Las Vegas professional development events.

I explained to Lee that a very small percentage of participants who attend presentations or seminars or who purchase personal development products actually see significant measurable results. I attribute this to being a passive consumer of information rather than an active creator of results.

Lee seemed very interested in our unique methodology that has its roots in the studies of accelerated learning and active training principles. I explained that by using a system that involves pre-event coaching in combination with a series of customizable active training on-site workshops, along with post-event follow-up e-mail and telephone coaching, we are able to track performance and guarantee results. Participants will walk away with their own personalized action plan for their success outcomes. Lee really liked the concept and wondered if our event would serve as a valuable follow-up to the many seminar-style Wake Up events. We agreed that an event of this nature would need to be limited to a small, elite group with a strong focus on personalized individual coaching and performance tracking.

Since that initial meeting, we decided to join forces, creating amazing possibilities.

On that day, a simple greeting in the men's restroom transformed into a venture of like-minded individuals—individuals who have created a team with the same vision and values on a mission to help create positive change in others.

Success begins with a decision to be successful! We attribute attracting the right opportunities to making clear decisions. You will attract what you put out into the universe.

Success is much easier when you take the "I" out of the equation and insert "we." You do not need to do it all yourself to be successful. Success is so much more satisfying when others benefit.

We now have a team made up of amazing people who share the efforts to help those who are willing to accept the challenge to wake up and live the life they love!

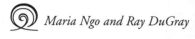 *Maria Ngo and Ray DuGray*

Victim or Victor
Bill Bartmann

Victim and victor: two six letter words that look so much alike, yet have entirely different meanings. If you happen to fit the description of one of these two words—victim—your world is a sad, unfair and hopeless place where you feel you have little or no control over the things that happen to you or around you. If you fit the description of the other word—victor—your world is full of exciting challenges and possibilities. You are the master of your own destiny and tomorrow is not feared, but anticipated with hope and excitement.

These two words and the people they describe are so different, one can't help but wonder why someone would choose to be a victim rather than a victor. "Choose?" you might be thinking. "Do you mean we get to make a choice?" Absolutely!

Whether you are a victim or victor is simply a product of one thing: *your view of the circumstances you now face.*

If our view of our present circumstances is one of sorrow, anger or hopelessness, then we have decided to become a victim. Once we feel sorry for ourselves, mad at someone else or hopeless because of an unfortunate situation, we have chosen to become a victim. When we have chosen to view our situation as one that we didn't cause or didn't deserve, and one we can't do anything about, we have agreed to become a victim. If, instead, our view of those same circumstances is one of accepting responsibility for our own actions, learning from the experience and assessing what we still have and what we can do about those circumstances, then we have decided to become a victor.

It is appropriate to feel sorrow, pity or even anger when something bad happens in our lives. Each of these emotions has a value and a utility in helping us deal with the calamities we face. These emotions help us go through the grieving process, but grieving is supposed to be a short-term process, not a permanent status. When that grieving starts to define who we are, we have allowed it to become a crutch—we have made a choice. We have decided that we would rather wallow in sorrow and self-pity and blame others for our predicament. We have chosen to become a victim.

Becoming a victim was the product of a choice we voluntarily made. Becoming a victor is also the product of a choice—one that is equally voluntary.

When calamity, tragedy, failure, losses or setbacks occur, we should grieve; we should allow our healthy emotions to run their course. But we should end our period of grieving as soon as possible. It should be our goal to complete our grief quickly—not to wallow in it—and we can shorten this period by taking control of the process. Here are some ways we can do so:

1. Engage in an honest assessment of what you did or did not do that has contributed to this circumstance.
The first step in becoming a victor instead of a victim is acknowledging this circumstance is a result of a decision that you made—not just something that "happened to you."

We are products of the decisions we make. Even when natural disasters strike, though we can't control them, we did make the decision to be in that geographic location at that particular time.

Now, does this make us stupid or cavalier? No! We made the decision to live in a location of our choosing because the positive attributes out-weighed the negative possibilities. But the choice was ours.

2. Endeavor to learn from the experience.
When we are in the midst of experiencing one of these unfortunate cir-

cumstances, it is hard to find any value in the experience. Yet, when looking back at previous calamities, the passage of time allows us to see the good that came out of them. If we honestly re-evaluate the worst things that have ever happened to us, most of us can find something positive that resulted from each of the experiences. As difficult as it is to see the good while we are in the middle of the situation, the sooner we look for it, the sooner we will find it.

3. Recognize what you still have and relish these things.
The easiest and best way to move from victim to victor is to look around you and take note of what you still have. During these moments of crisis it is natural to focus on what we have lost—after all, that is what crisis and calamity are all about. Instead of concentrating on what we've lost, we should focus our attention on what we still have.

4. Commit yourself to action to remedy (or alleviate) the situation.
The first step to overcoming a tragedy, loss or failure is to take control of the situation. As long as we allow the circumstances to control us— rather than the other way around—we will always be a victim, not a victor.

Here are some examples of people who chose to become victors, not victims:

- A hurricane Katrina survivor (notice I didn't use the media word "victim") who decided to rebuild bigger and better without blaming the mayor, the governor, FEMA or God.
- The mother who had the courage to forgive the man who murdered her only son.
- The unwed mother who refused to quit school because her baby needed a mother with income earning capacity.
- The loving husband who lost his wife of 36 years and then dedicated the balance of his life to making her proud of him by getting involved in her favorite charity.

- A man who lost his eyesight and then went on to create a television network for people who were blind.

Each of these people could easily have settled into the role of victim. If they had done so, most certainly we would have felt sorry for their situation and offered our pity. To the credit of these individuals, they did not want our sorrow or our pity. Nor did they want the title of victim. Each of them made a simple but profound choice; they chose instead to be a victor.

By choosing to be a victor, they chose a world full of exciting challenges and possibilities. They chose to be masters of their own destinies. They chose tomorrows that would be eagerly anticipated with hope and excitement. They demonstrated that it was their choice to make. On a regular basis, we, too, are presented the choice of being a victim or a victor. The question we must ask ourselves is, "Which will I choose?" The answer to that question and the result that will surely follow is simply up to us.

 *Bill Bartmann*

I AM DESIGNING MY LIFE, ARE YOU?
Jean M. Hiltner

My mind thought I was living the life I was destined to live, but my heart always knew better.

My parents divorced when I was young—perhaps that is not so unique, but nonetheless, we learned the important things from our grandparents. We always knew that Grandma would take care of the house while Grandpa went to work. I recall being at our grandparents' house at harvest time. Gram would pick pickles and can them, make apple pies and applesauce, and can green and yellow beans and beets. As children, we never thought much about the effort Grandma put into cooking and canning.

Years later, on my first night of cooking for my husband, I was using a canister set that had come from my step-dad's late mom. I made pork chops with cream of mushroom gravy. The gravy was runny, so I tried to thicken it with cornstarch, but it wasn't working; sure enough, I had used powdered sugar. My husband, Randy, tried to eat the pork chops, but they were terrible. I have improved in the kitchen since then.

I tell this story because, in my life thus far, it seems people just assume that others know how to do things. While some of us pretend we can do everything, deep inside, we are truly scared to the core.

All of my life I was searching; I wasn't sure of my goal, but I was searching. All the people in my life whom I thought were happy had ended up divorced or miserable. I had always wanted to travel the world, yet none of the people I was with were talking about it or doing it.

Randy and his buddies went on their hunting trips. I would tease them, saying they only hunt because "they cannot kill the woman, so they have to kill something." As my faith has grown, I have realized that is not something I should say. What we speak becomes our reality.

Consider this your warning: "Be careful of your words." The dear man I am married to allowed me to do and have anything that I wanted. I could not see that at the time, but I am glad I see it now.

Before we married in 1995, we went to the pastor of the church and asked for marriage classes. He told us we were old enough and didn't need them. Well, we have been in struggle mode ever since we said "I do." When Randy asked me to marry him, I had a choice: him and his house in Shafer, Minnesota, or my 1979 paid-off mobile home and the new Ford Explorer I intended to purchase. We did not consider creating more income because we had never been taught that way of thinking; we were taught that we had to choose one or the other.

In 1996, we decided it was time for us to have children. Both of my sisters had bad endrometreosis, and sure enough, I also followed suit. The doctors gave me a few options, but none were any we wanted to do. We wanted to try on our own. I was working for a small salon as well as part-time at a local factory. We did it, we were going to have a baby! When we found out the great news, my husband and I decided to open our own business. I love to do hair (and am very talented at it). I love to help people feel great about themselves, but as far as any business sense was concerned, I had none.

Everyone in our family was very supportive and did all they could to help. As the opening date neared, everything was almost done and my clients were waiting anxiously. But then the most unexpected thing happened: We went for my 12-week pregnancy check-up, and the doctor found no heart beat. He told us not to worry, and we scheduled an ultrasound—there was still no heartbeat. The baby had only developed to eight weeks. What a horrible day! I was so stubborn that instead of going home and losing the baby there, my mom stayed with me at the salon all day and I continued to see my clients. I write this because now I can see how little I valued myself. My total lack of respect for myself and our marriage continued until I finally found what I was searching for.

Do you know where the healing process started? Network marketing. The Lord brought exciting people into the salon who invited us to see what they were so excited about. We fell in love. Randy and I became excited for different reasons; he fell for the financial freedom, and I fell for the great people and the excitement. Money was not something I had ever desired. Randy, on the other hand, wanted to be debt-free. Until we started all the traveling and product buying, he was well on his way. He did a complete "180"—he always wanted to be debt-free, and then we saw a glimpse of this new and wonderful life.

The great people we met and the wonderful wellness products we were introduced to have assisted me in improving my health each year, and on Labor Day evening a few years ago, our lives changed for the better when our baby boy, Lance Lee Hiltner, was born. I was in so much denial prior to his birth that I still had not unpacked any of his clothes; we did not even have a crib set up. My wonderful sister took her precious time and did it all. My family planned his baptism. My whole life, I remember everyone helping me. As the years passed, we were blessed with another miracle, Hannah RoseMarie Hiltner. Again my wonderful sisters and our parents stepped in to help.

Now, our salon has been closed since June 2006, and we are finally developing a system of guidelines that we can all follow. I will not be one of those parents who screams at their children to pick things up when I don't have my own belongings put away. I have learned everything must have a place or you must not keep it. Keeping your life simple but exciting is the best thing for you.

We have accumulated four rental and investment properties. My sister asked me some time ago, "Why don't you close your business and assist your husband with his?" Smart woman, but at the time it was still about me; I chose not to hear her. Now that I am developing myself every day, with God by my side, I see how truly wise my sister is. We are currently in the process of building a multi-level million dollar network marketing empire. With all of the experience I've gained, I realize how important teamwork is in every area of your life. Now that we have taken the long, hard path that we were destined to take, it is our responsibility to share with the world that this wonderful thing called life is truly meant to be enjoyed. We will continue to close the doors that are still connected to the old ways and open the doors to all the new and exciting possibilities. I have learned one very important thing: Get back to basics and realize that you are a treasure and your body is God's temple. Remember to treat yourself that way. Since I have stepped back and looked in the mirror, I have realized I never took time to see who I was and where was I going. Now that I have, I know that it was worth everything we went through to get to where we are going.

Finally, I challenge you to truly look at yourself from head to toe today. Start looking just a little, then tomorrow look a little longer and truly see yourself the way others see you.

Take time to enjoy the life the Lord has chosen for you to live, and teach others to do the same.

 *Jean M. Hiltner*

POSITIVE MESSAGE OVERLOAD
Teagin Maddox

Have you ever wondered why there are so many people who have more than you? I am so sick of them. Most of us have tried to learn from them at some point, hoping we can repeat whatever they did so we can buy the same things they have.

They are the many self-helpers who make us feel like we don't know how to live or the countless personal growth gurus with their how-to books and the same goal of helping us become enlightened so we can have the life of our dreams. We are inspired, anxious to apply their techniques. But slowly, we drift back to our lives still just dreaming of fancy dinners and great vacations, their messages stuck in our heads. It isn't about possessions or money, they say—yeah, right.

We are turned off by this repetitive message because we want the truth—it *is* about money and material things. I *do* want the big house and the Bentley in the driveway; why can't I be enlightened *and* have stuff? Why is it that all those self-helpers who tell us not to want are the very people living in those places we love, driving those cars we desire?

It's easy for them to say, "Don't want this or that," because they already have it. How do we know they achieved their success by following their own advice anyway? And why would they say follow this system, but don't desire the things the system can bring? Maybe "the secret" is that what drove them to getting all that stuff was the very *lack* of stuff from which I now suffer. I think they owe us an explanation.

Why can't I start from wanting? Possessions and money are not evil things set on world destruction; yet, wanting them is apparently the cause of my too-small house. Telling me not to want does not end my desires, I hate to tell you. I still want that slammin' big house, Manolo Blahniks and hair extensions. Is that too much to expect out of my time here? The people on the podium who keep telling me to focus "within" need to understand that they aren't getting me anywhere fast enough. And I'm telling you, what's "within" is the longing for a big house, lots of money and more hair.

We original non-believers, or more precisely, those of us who prefer the ultimate American dream of overnight success, are looking for a prescription that leads us straight to the big house—literally. At every seminar we attend, with every page we read, the little voice in our heads screams: "Just tell us what you did already!"

We all want a quick fix. Then we could skip the tough stuff—the personal development and spiritual journeys that seem inseparable from the good things in life. But that requires time, patience and cash—the very things many of us lack until something catastrophic happens that forces us to find it. Then, find it we do.

When my daughter was diagnosed with scoliosis, I found time and money very quickly. I dragged her to every doctor, guru and spiritual healer I could find, searching for a fast repair before things got worse. The only promises came from surgeons. They had the quickest fix of all and the lowest interest in options, because they have hungry knives and bills to pay—but I was reassured that everything would probably turn out okay.

Denying surgery certainly mocked the quick-fix mentality. But morning, noon and night I researched options as my daughter's condition worsened. People said I was wasting time and giving her false hope, but actually, I was being patient, believing I would find another way despite the naysayers and the desire for an immediate result. Quick fixes are gimmicks—untruths—that lead us down a path we think will end at a pot of gold. Instead, the pot is empty and you have to start over again.

The successful people know that things happen when you combine belief with trust. They did not get into their big houses single-handedly, and I could not fix my daughter's spine alone. I surrounded myself with people and information that supported other solutions, and that set about a chain of events that changed my daughter's life forever.

The doctor I eventually found needed us as much as we needed him. We became a team—a team that believed in possibility, in the value of going against the protocol and against the surgery, which plays into the deceptively real American dream of the quick fix answer. The doctor needed a group of people who believed he could accomplish his goal, who believed in supporting him to find a way: *His* way. When his ideas were valued, his successes came, which allowed him to correct scoliosis even though everyone said it was impossible. Many people contributed to his ability to find the solution, including his patients, who were willing to believe. As we spread the word, his team will grow and people's lives will be changed. This is what the big house people are trying to do: Spread the message of things that work and teach us that every great result comes from hard work, dedication and persistence.

They know that teams become complete when many elements line up together and you begin to share your achievements with others through education. We must motivate others to believe that anything is possible, so that they, too, can impact the world somehow.

I live to encourage people to try options, to challenge the mentality of the quick fix we Americans want so badly. I've learned that sharing success isn't necessarily about the big house; that is simply a desirable side effect you may or may not want for yourself when you belong to a team of people that converge and make things happen for others. Picking a like-minded team of people to associate with and connect to is the answer to getting whatever you wish, whether it's a big house, a fancy car or a cure for a medical condition.

By joining a team who believes anything is possible and leaving the team of naysayers who see no options, you create options. This is where the big house people live, and they surround themselves with other big house people who try to show the other team the possibilities. Together, they try to tell us, "You can do this, too," and we disbelieve because their way requires work and dedication, just like my daughter's scoliosis treatment. If you persist, the big house and fancy car will come, but you probably won't care about it anymore.

My big house came when I watched my daughter's scoliosis reverse. The work it took was more valuable than any miracle or any quick fix. The combined insight and power of the team we were on brought us our desired result.

When you are aware of your beliefs, you will find the right team and you will get the results you crave. Beliefs and teams cannot be separated. One without the other simply doesn't work.

 *Teagin Maddox*

NEVER GIVE UP
Allan L. Roberts

The daily newspaper headline read: "£19,000 Debt Leads to Man's Suicide." I remember reading the headline and thinking, "Why? There is always someone to turn to for help."

Taking bad advice and giving control of my money to a financial adviser had reduced me from living in a luxury four-bed detached house to a three-bed semi-detached with £170,000 worth of debt. To make matters worse, my job had just been made redundant. My thoughts, however, were not on suicide, but on how to solve my problem.

My career had been in electro-mechanical engineering, but I had been working as a computer engineer, maintaining systems for a major bank. I headed for the employment center and was told that, because of my age, finding another job may be difficult. A few weeks passed, and my debts were spiralling out of control. I made agreements with most of my creditors, but there was still no sign of work, even though I applied for anything I felt capable of doing.

After a couple of years of struggling, a day or so before my 34th wedding anniversary, a knock on the door brought me even more problems—my wife was having an affair. When the reality of the situation finally hit me, I was so depressed I didn't know what to do. I could not think of a worse mess; it was like a nightmare.

I had no idea then that my troubles had only begun. My luxury home was gone, my money was gone, my job was gone, my trade was gone, my health was gone and my wife decided she would go, too. She moved out to stay with her new partner.

I loved my wife; I'd held her hand from the day we'd met. Heartbroken, I was left alone with my two daughters, who supported me as much as they were able. My dog, at this time my closest friend, died. Without money, I had been unable to have him treated by the vet. On top of all my troubles, this second heartache seemed like the end of the world.

With only unemployment and disability checks to live on, I could not afford to keep the house. I pleaded with my wife to keep the mortgage payments going until I could sell, but she stopped talking to me and refused to pay one penny toward the mortgage or the debts, even though they were in joint names.

When my house was sold, I was homeless. Deep in debt, unemployed, disabled and homeless, I went to the council for help and was told, "Tough." They will only help you if you are pregnant. I could not believe it. I was being turned away with only some extra housing points for being disabled.

With nowhere to live, I slept in a plastic tunnel used for horticulture. Everything was damp, there was no form of heating and ice would form overnight on the plastic. I understood that if you are suffering from hypothermia you must stay awake or you may die. Some nights, I would cry myself to sleep, desperate to escape the pain in my legs from diabetes, cold and hunger, not worrying if I would wake in the morning.

I managed to get a motor home with no interior, which allowed me to sleep off the ground but was still cold. My unemployment had been stopped, so I had no money for food. I lived on two to three meals per week, making up the rest of the time with a packet of biscuits and cups of tea made on a camping stove. In four months, I lost more than 50 pounds and lacked energy to do anything.

But my luck began to change; I was given a one-bed flat by a housing association. At Christmas, my children joined together and bought me a cooker and some food, and I was able to cook Christmas dinner for them. It was my first proper meal since losing my house.

The same month, due to the tireless efforts of a lady at the employment center who helped and encouraged me through my troubles, I started a new job.

By April, I had managed to create a routine and organize where my money had to go. I made a decision that I was never going to go through all those difficulties again. I bought myself a computer and a mind-mapping program, and I mapped out all my plans for the future, all my goals and how I was going to achieve them. I set out daily routines, weekly targets, monthly targets and yearly targets. My five-year plan was to make a million pounds.

Eighteen months in and slightly ahead of my target, I had another setback. I was rushed to the hospital for a major operation which put me out of work for six months and left me about a year behind on my plan. I basically had to start again.

Three years after my wife moved out, she left her partner. He had put her deep into debt and she didn't have enough wages to cover repayments. My daughters persuaded her to come talk to me, and I was able to restructure her payments so that they would be paid off quickly, while still giving her some money to spend. It was the same system I had created to clear my debts. Our divorce became final exactly 39 years after we were married. Our marriage is over, but we are talking now and have the occasional cup of tea; instead of remaining distant or bitter about the situation, I have chosen to remain on her team to help her learn the lessons I've learned.

I felt as if I had been at sea in a storm and had now reached safety. I wonder about the man who thought £19,000 was too big of a set-back to withstand. Where was his support system? Having had real life experience, I can help others who have found themselves in difficult situations. I have joined a couple of support groups and am now creating my own Web site, www.roughseasafeharbour.com. I had never written a book, but now I have a motivational book at a publisher and have also created a personal development course which will soon be available on my Web site. I believe anyone can overcome life's complexities with a little bit of support, understanding and compassion from the right people—the right teammates.

I feel my life is now growing in leaps and bounds. Money is no longer my main goal, although it is beginning to head my way again. I can already see my million on the horizon. I know that if I can help enough people learn to look beyond their problems, never hold a grudge and never, never give up, I will reach my goal. I want to be a positive influence on my team—the group of people who will come and go in my life; I know I can teach them that anything is possible. I am looking forward to living out my days in a little cottage by the sea with a new dog for company and the personal satisfaction of knowing that I didn't give up.

 *Allan L. Roberts*

THE BERMUDA TRIANGLE AND BEYOND
Bill King

I was trapped; trapped in a city I loathed, a profession that was killing me and a life that was at a dead end. Fear was controlling my life, and I always had a standard response to it: avoidance. The choices I made kept me from having to face my fears, but they also kept me from realizing my dreams.

I had been claustrophobic as long as I could remember, and then I developed a fear of flying. When I was 8 years old, I almost drowned. This fear of water led to a fear of bridges, which led to a fear of heights.

My loving wife decided she would help me take baby steps toward conquering my many phobias. She managed to find the shortest cruise in history, from Fort Lauderdale to the Bahamas. That covered my fear of flying, claustrophobia and water—yep, she had just about gotten them all into one trip! I cringed as she explained that her gift to commemorate our 10 years of marriage was to kill me on a doomed flight or drown me at sea.

"You can do it, honey! It's only six hours!" Her eyes were filled with hope and excitement, but all I heard was an eerie tune from my childhood. *"Just sit right back and you'll hear a tale, a tale of a fateful trip. A six hour tour, a six hour tour."*

The morning of the cruise was filled with ominous signs. First was the rain—lots of it. We had to run through it after being told to "walk the plank" to the ship. Easels at every doorway proclaimed, "Warning, rough seas. Take necessary precautions." Deviously, my wife pushed me past each one, toward the biggest breakfast buffet on the planet where I ate like it was my last meal.

As I rolled my bloated belly to the upper deck, the staff lined the handrails with seasick bags. A voice in my head screamed, "Get me off this thing!" But we had already left the port.

The high seas tossed the 190-foot ship around like a toy boat in a bathtub. We tried to get out of the cold, but the seasick bags inside were in full use. My body shook violently with fear, but at least outside I could blame it on the weather.

My nausea began to rise to serious levels. In the movies, you see people get sick in public all of the time, but when it happens for real it's a whole different story. Embarrassed, humiliated and with tears in my eyes, I glared at the spectators like Maximus in *Gladiator*. "Are you not entertained?"

I began thinking in segments—if we could just stay afloat for four more 30-minute segments we might survive. And finally, land! Thank you, God! But something was wrong; we were going the wrong way! Then came the worst possible announcement: "We have been advised that the seas are too rough for us to enter port. For the safety of the passengers, we have been advised to turn back." Safety of the passengers? Turn back?

Despite my fear of water, I stared at the island in the distance, trying to calculate the odds that I would be able to swim to it. I actually took a step toward the edge, thinking my chances of survival were better if I jumped. But as the land disappeared, my hope was gone.

After more than eight hours of putting it off, I couldn't wait any longer to use the restroom. The ship swayed back and forth so badly that I hit my head on all four walls of the stall. The seas went from 25 feet to 35 feet to 45 feet to 55 feet! Each wave got higher and higher, and after 12 hours of being tossed about, the air began to feel different. Fear gripped the ship, and silence prevailed.

Now, too frightened to even open my eyes, I sat on the floor inside the ship and hooked my arm around the leg of a table. I understood for the very first time why I was forced to memorize prayers as a child. I repeated the prayers as I went deeper inward; the fear around me faded away.

We later learned that we actually sailed through the earliest tropical storm ever recorded. We had survived 65-foot waves and sustained 70-mile-per-hour winds. Someone on our ship had died and many more were taken to the hospital.

I am neither a statistician nor a gambler, but trying to calculate the odds of being on that ship, on that day, in that tropical storm made me believe that there was a reason I was in that place, at that time.

I did nothing about it for at least six months, but then started evaluating my life and began daily affirmations. Within a few short months, I found the job of my dreams in a large city and faced many of my other fears. If I could make it through that cruise, I could make it through anything.

For about 10 years after that incident, I immersed myself in self-help publications. I then asked God, "How can I serve?" I asked it many times every day for three weeks. One day, while doing my morning meditation, I kept getting one great idea after another. Annoyed, I thought, "I am trying to make a connection to God. Please be quiet!" I struggled with this for a while, when suddenly a blank slate appeared in my mind. Instantly, I stopped thinking. A few seconds later the word "WRITE" appeared in bold black letters.

I finally got the message and quickly went to my computer to begin writing. In only three days, I wrote a book and presented it to several young adults and their friends. I also wrote companion books for adolescents and their parents. I have continued writing and haven't slowed down since.

I began giving seminars and coaching young adults. I started a new company and have finally found my life's purpose. So, what began as a tragedy turned out to be a blessing. In getting me onto that ship, my wife forced me to face my deepest fears—in doing so, I was transformed. I am free! A good teammate brings out the best in the team, as my wife was able to bring out the best in me.

Now I am excited about what the universe and I can create together. And though I may still feel fear sometimes, I now interpret those fears as a sign that I need to re-evaluate my thoughts. I will never again let them keep me from doing exactly what I want to do!

 Bill King

BLESS THIS WORLD, IT'S BIGGER THAN ME
Monica Jordan

We must ask, believe, receive and move forward. If we focus on our unlimited dreams and make promises to ourselves with a positive attitude, we can achieve our goals! Let go of your fears. Build a well thought-out foundation of faith, family, friends and forgiveness. Build business with integrity. Decide what makes you happy, then go for it.

Our own fears, uncertainties and lack of self-confidence keep us where we are—bored, unchallenged, unhappy and afraid. The benefits are win-win: Help those around you as you share your vision, and lift yourself up as well. Stop worrying about what others think and begin to knock down the restraints you have put on yourself. Change your environment and surround yourself with supportive people who are smarter than you. Think huge—don't limit yourself. Allow yourself to touch base with those limitless dreams you had as a kid, before life got in the way. Start asking questions, visualize your direction, focus, enjoy the journey and achieve.

When my dream materialized, I had been living in a cozy fourth-floor walk-up apartment. I had worked steadily for 14 years in telecommunication customer service and sales, but still struggled financially. I was unappreciated; I only worked there for the money. I knew there was more, but I was unable to connect the dots. I would pat myself on the back every day, attempting to motivate myself to get up and go into work. I made the decision to be there, stayed positive and focused, and I grew as a result. Few customers could shake me; I put myself in their shoes each time to resolve their complaints and it worked. I was learning. I was high-school educated, but experientially smart. I took 50 to 70 customer calls a day, and five to six of them were randomly recorded each month. Consistently, two to three of those calls would score a 100 percent award-winning customer service. That was great; I won a lot of awards. Work was challenging and it was nice to be recognized, but the praise was empty. I was unappreciated. They had forgotten that their staff members were customers too. I knew there was more.

While working in telecommunications, I performed stand-up comedy for 12 years. Originally, it was sexually-based comedy, and later, as I grew, it became more day-to-day observations with clean, funny stories and twists. I toured western Canada and had a great time, but the travel cost me more money than I was making, and my financial situation was not improving. Other performers and entertainers were making it; where was I going wrong? I wanted to work smart, not hard. I decided to go for it and quit my job. I was in debt, but I had saved up enough money to cover my expenses, allowing me the time to invest in *me*. Now, that's one giant step when you believe. For a year and a half I kept things low-key, staying at home to write my one-woman show. Unfortunately, I lost focus, got bored and was not gaining any headway. I took on a temporary job as a receptionist at the local newspaper. It paid well with great hours, but the shine wore off quickly and I became bored again.

On my second-to-last day working there, a reader called in and asked me to find an article in the previous day's paper. It was about an introductory evening event, the Canadian version of *Rich Dad, Poor Dad*. I had found the dots! I bought the books and attended the seminars and began learning about real estate investing, developing businesses, building and achieving with integrity, becoming an entrepreneur and building a championship team. That was it! I had been holding myself back and thinking too small. The biggest difference between me and so many others who had been given these opportunities was that I took action and believed in myself with passion. It was time to really get in the game.

There was one investment opportunity that hit home: building a telecommunication WiFi network across North America. The minimum investment was $100,000. I stood up in a room of 250 people and said I was going to create a joint venture with my $40,000 (from cash in retirement funds) and go for it. It was exciting; I was passionate and surrounded by support—I got 59 business cards over the two-day

investment opportunity. I hired lawyers and re-wrote WebNet Global contracts, opened the company and spent $28,000 on legal bills.
I raised $1 million in five months with projected returns of well more than 200 percent, all on my own dime. WebNet Global was so pleased they hired me to do it again.

I work from home and represent more than 400 investors and 24 licenses, having raised more than $7 million. I am paid commission when people invest, but volunteer on the board of directors to make it a win-win for four of my companies. Without me, it would not have gotten started; that is a big achievement.

I am thankful for these experiences and have been blessed! Through prayer, hard work, passion and focus, I have built the foundation for my championship team. I created my own job: CEO, entrepreneur and president of five successful companies. I started slow, laying the foundation to build my team. My dreams were bigger than me and I began to realize that if I surrounded myself with a team of focused, like-minded thinkers, anything would be possible!

I have begun my exit strategy for stepping down as president from four of the boards while believing that passionate investors will successfully take over my role. I will continue to work for WebNet in licensing and will focus my time on my personal business—consulting and motivational and inspirational speaking—which has been on hold. I'm starting slowly, building my foundation and championship team and realizing my limitless dreams. It has been an amazing year and a half. My salary has increased 10-fold, I own a home and a new car, and I am blessed with great family and friends. I am 37 years old and full of love, faith and belief. I am happy, I am at peace and I have only begun to scratch the surface of what I can achieve. You can, too!

 *Monica Jordan*

FROM BUILDING A TEAM TO BUILDING YOUR DREAMS
Dr. Charles Majors

Ninety-nine percent of you reading this will not make it to age 60 in good health! The frightening truth is that our children will be the first generation to die before their parents. Let me prove that to you right now. Who do you know who's over 60, in great health, on no medications? The answer is almost no one! You probably have the same thought they did—"It's not going to happen to me"—but the reality is that you're already on your way!

When I was a senior in high school, I watched my grandmother die right in front of me. I watched my mother kiss her goodbye, but cancer had already taken her life. As I took my turn to kiss her and say my last words, there was an awareness that sparked in me—we shouldn't have to lose our loved ones at such a young age or watch them suffer. We were created to live to age 120 not 40 on drugs, depressed, diseased and dead by 65!

At the time, I was a C student, but I began applying myself fully and working as hard as I could to get where I wanted to go. My mom raised me to believe that I could do anything I wanted, whatever it was. She said that it didn't matter if I was a C student, I would succeed if I was dedicated to the goal. Sure enough, I got into a top university, went from there to chiropractic school and graduated successfully. When I first graduated from college, everything didn't fall into my lap. I wasn't immediately living my dream. I started slowly, and as things continued to move at that pace, I realized that I needed a team—that's when my vision started to take off. Once you learn that someone ahead of you has already accomplished great things along the path you wish to follow, you understand that it is near foolishness to do it on your own.

After that, I began forming the team that would take me to the great places I wanted to go. I knew that, in order for me to reach my goal of saving and changing people's lives, I would need an outstanding team of individuals who wanted the same thing, and many of whom had been there and done that already. I realized that I needed to model people who already did what I wanted to do.

I sought out two coaches for each area of my life and work so that I could accelerate my success. I found the professionals who were already doing what I wanted to do, coaches who were promoting the ideas of the "Maximized Living" program and helping thousands of patients. I also hired two financial coaches and a life coach. So, from the very beginning, I've always had a team that's been behind me, supporting my vision and getting me to my goal as quickly as possible. These coaches supported me, pushed me and helped me grow.

Now, with the help of that supportive team, I am a "Maximized Living" chiropractor, traveling the country and presenting seminars on how living your life by five maxims will take you to your fullest, healthiest potential. I teach people how to eat God's way, how to maximize oxygen supply, how to lose the medications they think they are dependent upon, how to manage stress and how to keep their nervous system clear of interference.

My vision today is a global one. I have a goal that every human being will come to understand how to live the "Maximized Living" lifestyle and reach their full life potential of 120 years, in the way that God intended for us—with health, wealth and strong relationships.

These maxims can work for children and adults alike, as well as for the sick and the comparitively healthy. Through our seminars and in our offices, we do extreme life makeovers with the same steps: Clear the nervous system, focus on the exact nutritional needs of the body, get the right amount of oxygen through proper exercise, de-stress, and educate on the dangers of medications. With the final step, we literally reverse the toxicity and take the toxins out of a person's body. We teach people how to stay truly healthy for a lifetime. We transform lives and help people create health in every area, from physical to relationships, self-actualization and nutrition.

The patients I treat are often living under extreme circumstances. Some are autistic children, some have only 30 days to live. Others have tried everything to improve their health, but nothing has worked. What we teach them is that other programs have failed because they do not address complete health. By only fixing one or two of the issues, they leave holes in a leaking ship. The "Maximized Living" protocol focuses on every area of health, which is why it always works.

Now, as I travel the country presenting these seminars, I am constantly aware that I would not be where I am today—teaching these maxims and informing others about how to live a fuller, healthier life—if it weren't for the team I pulled together in the beginning. Almost all of the coaches and team members I began with are still part of my life, working with me and teaching me.

Now I am a successful "Maximized Living" practitioner, I'm a success coach to hundreds, and I've built one of the largest natural healthcare clinics in the world. I have teams forming behind me that are using the steps that I've taken as their example, just as I used the steps of those who came before me. I learned first how to follow, and now I am learning how to lead. I'm no different than you. If you set your mind to it, focus and get the right team and coaches, you can build the life of your dreams.

Dr. Charles Majors

MULTIPLE SCLEROSIS STOLE
MY PIANO BUT NOT MY LIFE
Diane McLaren

Even as I am trying to put this story into words, reliving those moments is excruciating. I do not want to remember—my eyes well up with tears, my heart gets very tight, my breathing gets shallow and quickens. I am holding my breath. I close my eyes and debate continuing. A tear is on my cheek. It still hurts so much just to remember.

In 1982, I was living my dream far from home, attending Montreal's McGill University, majoring in music and loving every second of it. I couldn't get enough—theory, harmony, history, great composers, great teachers. Even the study and practice was interesting. I was only 19 and was going to be a classical pianist and teacher. Life was good!

Then my eyesight began to fade. I began seeing double and started to lose control of my right arm and hand. In what seemed like an instant, everything went terribly wrong. I couldn't brush my hair or my teeth because my fingers did not work and my arm wouldn't cooperate. I couldn't dress myself. My right leg began to fail; it was dragging behind me. Then things got worse.

I was in the hospital, my right side totally paralyzed from my shoulder to my toes. Nothing was moving and the left side of my face was paralyzed. My brain knew what to do, but everything had been disconnected and I felt imprisoned. I couldn't even express myself verbally because of facial paralysis.

This was my first major multiple sclerosis crisis. Lying in that hospital bed, I was exhausted all the time, with numbing pain, failing bladder control and a colon that had essentially shut down. "Why me?" I thought.

After months of countless tests, the doctors delivered their diagnosis:

Multiple Sclerosis. "We do not know why or how you got it and there is no cure," they told me. "You might regain 75 percent leg function, 50 percent arm and hand function and some speech, but we do not know if or when. We should tie your tubes to avoid children and you'll never play the piano or work full-time." This would have been bad news for anyone.

"Why me?" I kept thinking as I heard their words. I couldn't believe somebody so full of life, ambition and goals could be given this life sentence. I knew they had medically confirmed the diagnosis, but I didn't want to believe everything the doctors were telling me. I wanted to believe that in 10 to 15 years there'd be a cure for MS, or that somewhere in the world there were other doctors, alternative health therapies or medicines available to help.

The fact that my doctors did not know of any alternatives did not mean there was nothing available, so I refused to give up hope. That choice left me alone, and there were times when I felt low and discouraged. I started to believe it would be much easier to just give in, but I did not. Those doctors simply weren't ready to work as a team with me—I was determined to find people who would.

I remember being alone in that hospital more than once, sitting in a wheelchair and needing to use the bathroom. I could not transfer myself from the chair to the toilet, but I tried anyway. Falling on the floor, I waited a long time before being found. I hated to wait for help. I felt so powerless, so dependent. I could not bear the thought of being like that for the rest of my life! I had planned to live a full life; I was only 19! I fiercely wanted to walk again, to run, to ski and skate, and I certainly wanted to play my beloved piano.

Every day for months, I would close my eyes and imagine my life in the future, never seeing myself growing old in that wheelchair. I always saw myself as active and healthy. On the seat of that wheelchair, I pictured a bed of nails, and when my bottom would touch them, I'd jump to my feet.

I tried to share these thoughts, but the doctors believed I was in denial. "I understand I have MS," I told them. "But I will walk again, play piano and live the life I choose."

They sent me to a psychologist who told me I had better accept the facts of the situation. I told him about the pictures in my head, that there must be alternative treatments or medicines. He referred me to another psychiatrist and I repeated my dreams to deaf ears.

I made my choice and resolved to take the risks and search for the answers, despite their grim prognosis. Twelve months later, I was largely recovered with the help of some wonderful new teammates, Western medications and alternative therapies—but it didn't last.

By 1992, I'd built a life, married, given up on the music major, acquired a CMA degree, settled in the Toronto area, acquired a good job and had a healthy 2-year-old daughter. Life had been good, but I was now suffering a third debilitating MS crisis. This time, 12 months into it I was not sure I would ever come back.

Nothing was working and I was losing the fight. I called my mom one night in tears to tell her I was quitting everything because even the alternatives did not seem to be working anymore. It had been a year of minor progress, then regression, and I told her I was resigning myself to everyone's predictions.

But that night, something clicked. The next morning I called my mom back and told her I was back on the program; I would not quit and wait for a miracle or for my life to come crumbling down. I told her I had tried the Western medication without success, but I would continue with the natural remedies until I found something better. At least they had no serious side-effects.

Around that time, I was offered a handicapped license plate to simplify parking, but refused to take it because I would not accept that I was handicapped. I was determined to return to a normal life and again pictured my future self as healthy and active, but this time the picture was of running to catch my 2-year-old and rolling in the green grass beneath a perfect blue sky. I imagined the sweet smell of newly cut grass, our laughter, the birds singing and the rustle of wind in the leaves.

That's when I chose to aggressively pursue alternative therapies, nutritional supplements and education until I found someone or something that worked. Six months later, I was almost symptom-free and have never looked back! I continued training in the alternative health field and my family doctor has been very supportive, telling me not to stop whatever I was doing, because it was working.

While it began out of necessity, alternative health has become my life's passion. I have enjoyed symptom-free health since the early '90s, and developed a simple holistic solution to health for myself, and then my husband and my two beautiful, healthy daughters. Since 1994, I have counseled and educated my clients, students and partners.

My journey through life has been challenging, as have the journeys of others. But I believe just about everyone can achieve better health if they learn how. I still play the piano, but MS changed the course of my life. Today my mission is to be the advocate for others that my doctors did not initially want to be for me. Now, as a supportive teammate to those in need, I educate people on the choices they have available, then guide and motivate each to choose their own journey toward a lifetime of exceptional health and wellness.

Within each of us, nature has provided all the pieces necessary to achieve extreme health and wellness, then left it up to us to put them all together!

 *Diane McLaren*

WE ARE ALL JUST ONE BIG TEAM
Tatiana Escalada

From the moment I was born, I was Daddy's little girl. I was his pride and joy. He was my friend, my teammate, my dad, my hero and my mentor. We used to spend hours staring at the sky, making up characters and stories from the clouds. Singing funny songs and clowning around were his favorite ways to make me laugh, and I loved to sit for hours on end listening to his fascinating stories. He had lived an incredible life. He made me see life as a magical journey on which we embarked with a sense of discovery and amusement. The spirit of teamwork filled everything we did, and through it I was learning precious lessons, though I didn't know it at the time. Big or small, he was involved in all of my life's projects, dreams or quests—from trying to understand why the moon is round and doesn't fall from the sky to searching for the meaning of life and our purpose in this world. He was there to be my teammate on every occasion. Even if he knew the answers to my questions, very seldom would he give them to me; instead, he would get on my level, become a kid again and come up with all kinds of creative, crazy answers and theories. When I didn't buy any of them, he would say something like "Okay, you caught me. I don't know the right answer, but why don't we find out?"

As a team, we would embark on a very fun search. He showed me that the journey to the answer is just as important as finding it, because on the way, we will make unexpected discoveries. Those discoveries are made richer if we are with a friend or teammate.

Teamwork was engrained in him; it was his philosophy and motto. "We are a team," he would say. "Your mother, you and I are a team."

We were, and he was the best player on our team. Whether it was masterminding, researching information, inspiring and cheering me on or just standing back and giving me moral support, my father was always there for me.

Unfortunately, as I grew older, my mother and I were in a constant war, despite my father's efforts to keep our team united. I grew depressed, bitter and rebellious, which only got worse after my high school sweetheart passed away in a motorcycle accident. I was almost 18, but I felt old and dead inside, like an empty shell. Suicidal thoughts haunted my mind, and the only thing stopping me was imagining the pain it would cause my father. Reading and writing became my healing tools, supplemented by long conversations with my dad. After a few years, when I had regained strength and everything seemed to be going well, the unexpected happened—my father became ill. At first we thought it was something minor—Dad had always enjoyed great health and made sure the family got regular check-ups. But before we knew it, my father had lost 100 pounds and was in extreme pain. Exam after exam, doctors couldn't figure out what was wrong.

Even though seeing him in so much pain was killing me, I knew I had to be strong so that I could be there for him. Long walks became part of our daily routine and we read together and talked about books, movies and life. I went to the doctor with him and my mother and I made sure he followed his treatments. Slowly but surely, with a few stumbles along the way, my dad began to heal. He remained well for two glorious years. But then he got sick again. For more than seven long years we fought sickness and death. We didn't win, but the important thing is that we fought with all we had. As you can imagine, I was devastated. A big part of me died with him.

I have had many "wake up" moments in my life. Some have been subtle, others were drastic, but nothing compares to my father's death. Seeing my father fight for his life the way he did made me love him even more, and I found a new appreciation for life. I began to be thankful for every minute I am alive, for everything I have been able to give, for every lesson I've learned, for every time I have loved, for every tear and every smile. I learned that only true love makes effective teamwork flourish—love for what you do, for your teammates and also love for life, a passion for learning and sharing.

The Power Of Team

Love gives us the ability to let go of our egos and be a part of something bigger than ourselves; a union for a cause, a communion with others. When we understand that we are part of a whole, it doesn't matter who knows more or who is stronger; what matters is that we put our assets to work for the team's benefit. That is what teamwork is all about. My father's love for people, nature and life taught me to view the universe as a big team where everyone and everything is interdependent. We are all part of this team we call "earth," and everything we do has an effect on it.

Throughout our lives, our teams may face great challenges, like the ones my family had to face for seven painful, yet insightful, years of illness that ended my dad's life. The important thing is that, through our challenges, we find a way to pass on the lessons we have learned so that we can perhaps offer someone else an inspiring thought, a discovery or a magic moment that reminds us that life is bigger than we will ever understand.

Nowadays, I live a peaceful life in a place overlooking the bay where I can share beautiful sunsets with people I love. I direct a company I founded out of the need to do something more meaningful that provides tools and information products to improve people's lives. My mom is my upstairs neighbor and I see her every day. As for my dad, he still is my best teammate; when the sun shines, I like to think it's his smile shining down on me.

 *Tatiana Escalada*

SPEAK IT INTO EXISTENCE
Jason and Wanetta Gill

D id you know that thoughts are things? Obviously you cannot touch, feel or hold thoughts in your hands when they first develop. It takes continuous contemplation of a thought to begin the process of turning it into reality. After playing the thought over and over again in your mind, the next step is to speak the words out loud to yourself as well as to others, full of emotion and unquestioning belief. It must be backed with massive action until you are able to speak the thought into existence. My wife and I have experienced this extraordinary event firsthand on many occasions.

Wanetta Starts Her Journey and Leaves North Carolina

I have always been a "go-getter" and thought that I wanted to make a difference. After graduating from college in 1987, I immediately entered the career world. I quickly found I was not interested in sitting behind a desk for the rest of my life! I proceeded to get my real estate license, started working part-time at my uncle's dental practice and began a network marketing business, all while working another full-time job. Even with four jobs, I still needed financial help from my family from time to time. Being concerned, they saw all of my efforts and told me to stop working so hard. "We know you want to succeed, but that's not easy to come by," they said.

One day, I decided that I wanted to make a six-figure income and it wasn't going to happen to me there. I stepped out on faith, packed my bags and decided to move to Maryland. My family thought I was crazy, moving to a city where I really didn't know anyone. They told me I would have a hard time becoming successful. "You will be back," they said.

The only people I knew in Maryland were my cousin Byron, who was attending college, and my friend Larry, who I knew from my first network marketing business. I had to motivate myself daily, repeating with great emotion, "I can do it, I will earn a six-figure income, I will be successful."

After working diligently with my network marketing business for more than two years and using positive self-talk along with self-development, I was earning more than $85,000 a year. By this time I had listened to countless self-development tapes by dynamic speakers, read numerous books and was able to replace my full-time job as a legal secretary, where I was earning $50,000 a year. Finally, I had begun to have some success and could vividly see results.

The Bible says, *"And be not conformed to this world; but be ye transformed by the renewing of your mind"* (Rom. 12:2, KJV).

The renewing of the mind comes from putting positive information in our minds all of the time.

Jason Meets Wanetta
When I met my wife for the first time, it was not in person; I met her picture first. The year was 1997 in Dallas, Texas. I was at a network marketing convention and met a young lady from Virginia named Teresa. We exchanged business cards. As she was inserting my card into her business card rolodex, I happened to see Wanetta's business card with her picture on it.

"Wow, she is really pretty," I thought. "I wonder if she is single."

I took a chance and asked Teresa who she was. She said it was her friend Wanetta. I asked if she was single.

Teresa responded, "Yes, she is."

I then found myself telling Teresa that I wanted to meet her. After the convention, Teresa went home, called Wanetta and told her that she met a really nice guy who wanted to meet her. Wanetta said she wasn't interested.

Teresa said, "You don't understand, he is really nice and he is from New York."

Wanetta responded, "I definitely am not interested in meeting someone from New York, I'm from North Carolina."

But after a little arm-twisting from Teresa, Wanetta agreed to give me a call. We arranged to meet in person at our next convention in New Jersey in February of 1998.

When I finally met her, she gave me a big hug. At that very moment, God spoke to my spirit, revealing that she was going to be my wife. After that event, we started to speak on a regular basis over the phone, but she was not interested in anything more than friendship. One day after talking on the phone, I got so emotionally charged that I decided to put my words on tape congratulating her on an upcoming speech she had to present. After congratulating her, I mentioned that I had been praying and speaking to the Lord about bringing someone special into my life and that I knew that He sent her to me. I even told her that we were going to prosper together as a family. When she started listening to the tape, she did not even get halfway through before she stopped it and told her roommate, Robyne, "This guy must be crazy—he doesn't even know me."

More than four years passed with us still speaking constantly over the phone, but seeing very little of each other in person. She was still only interested in friendship. My thoughts and speech stayed the same, that one day Wanetta would be my wife. Then one day it happened. I asked her to go on vacation to Florida as I had every year, and for the first time, she said, "Yes." When her plane landed, she had about a 45-minute wait until my plane arrived.

She began to speak to the Lord, and she asked, "Lord, what am I doing here? I don't like this guy in an intimate way and I don't want to hurt his feelings," she thought. "He is one of my best friends."

The Lord spoke to her and said, "He is your husband."

She cried in the airport and let me know what the Lord had told her. A year later we were married.

Today we have used this principle of speaking thoughts into existence in all areas of our lives. We have truly prospered together in mind and spirit. We have acquired more than $4 million in real estate and have a very profitable network marketing business with distributors nationwide. Our income soared to half a million dollars in 2006, and we are on our way to helping thousands of people live the life they've always dreamed of.

These experiences have allowed us to understand that you can speak things into existence, but it is always on God's timetable, not ours. The Bible says, *"And all things, whatsoever ye shall ask in prayer, believing, ye shall receive"* (Matt. 21:22, KJV).

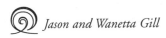 *Jason and Wanetta Gill*

FROM THE BOTTOM TO THE TOP
Yvon Laplante

When I was a young boy, my adoptive parents were very poor. We did not have enough food for three meals a day. My father had Parkinson's disease and my mother was handicapped, but I have always been a big dreamer. I told my mother I wanted to be someone people would like to be around.

At 9 or 10 years old, I became a gang leader, organizing all kinds of *events*, as we said in our language. "Doing some business," we called it. There were about 40 of us who met to organize our strategy for the weekend. Later, I became the leader of a motorcycle gang, and we did what gangs do.

Later, I began another group. We travelled around the world playing hockey and representing a worldwide company. During this time, I visited 80 countries and circled the world eight times. My goal was always to be a leader. I wanted people to follow me, but I didn't know how to do that. I was told that I was not intelligent. Without an education, I was always told, I would end up on the poor side of society. I did not let any of these warnings affect me. I strove toward my goal of leadership, but I still didn't know how to do that.

I was married for 22 years with no children. That did not work for me either; we were not from the same walk of life. The divorce was a wake-up call for me; the minute it was final, I got my dream back.

In 1988, I met two people who wanted to partner with me in business. I didn't know why they chose me, but I said yes. The business was to sell frozen chickens, and since I had contacts from around the world, I sold them at a rate of 25 containers per month. One day, I got a call from a customer telling me there was something wrong. He said one container had rocks in the middle to inflate the weight. So, I had to pay back the entire amount of the credit letter—that cost me $1.2 million. I had to sell everything I had: three properties, my house and the entire $340,000 in my bank account. I was broke again.

I thought, "What did I fail to do that I should have done?" Then it came to me. I had given too much of my power to my crooked partners—I now understood why they wanted to work with me. So, having lost everything, I began to look for a way to become successful again.

I started reading everything I could get my hands on. I read more than 600 books and attended more than 80 seminars to get started.

Then I met a great man. His name was Thomas Leonard, and he was the one who introduced me to coaching.

I joined a company that specialized in transformation. It was there where I discovered my many talents. After 10 years, I left to start my own company.

For the past seven years, I have been developing a new way for people to live their lives with power and freedom. My training has inspired me to seek to gain knowledge about people and their pain. I have also realized that there is good in every person.

Today, my company has five full-time coaches and 20 in training. We have created a technology that keeps people in action, and I have given more than 1,000 seminars, most of them in French. I now teach people how to win in their lives and share all my knowledge and experience from my own life.

It has also become clear to me what I want to do in life. I know that the more you learn and the more you train yourself, the easier it is to have access to yourself. There is always an opportunity out there waiting for you.

I have learned that I should not get upset over small things. I gave up the need to be in control, but I respect my own integrity. I also discovered that knowing everything is impossible, but learning from others gives me freedom and a powerful way of living. I have finally realized that any person who is willing to love people exactly as they are has an edge over anything that may come at him in life.

I believe that when you love to help other people win, you become surrounded by kind, loving people. When people take action with hope and the support of friends, they will forget their pain and start living again. Their self-esteem and self-confidence grow as they realize they have a life to live.

From gangs, to sports, to partners, I've learned that choosing a strong, supportive team is essential to making it to the top.

 *Yvon Laplante*

SUMMER: FRIEND OR FOE?
Vicki F. Panaccione, Ph.D.

The lights have been left on, the fan's on high and 3 a.m. giggles come from the computer room as video games blast and DVDs blare. Doritos wrappers, popcorn bowls, Gatorade jugs and remnants of homemade ice cream concoctions litter the family room. What's a mother to do? For some, it's time to pull their hair out and spend hours barking orders or picking everything up themselves. For me? I was savoring every moment. It was summer break—and Alex was home!

When my only child went away to college in August of 2004, it was, in a word, rough. After years of soccer games, band concerts, academic bowls, science fair projects, school plays, field trips, cupcakes and bake sales, tennis matches, baseball play-offs, award ceremonies, book fairs, music rehearsals, youth orchestra, honor society and on and on, life as I knew it was over.

It is amazing how different everything was without him. The house was quiet, clothes and towels weren't strewn around the bathroom, I could see his bedroom floor and there was no need to nag about taking out the garbage, cleaning the pool or emptying the dishwasher. This sounds like every mother's dream, but be careful what you wish for! I was miserable—which is why, when he once again filled the house with the noise and clutter of youth, I was delighted.

By no means am I advocating irresponsible behavior. Of course, children need to be taught to turn off lights, pick up after themselves, turn down the volume, "Et cetera, et cetera, et cetera," as the King of Siam once said. I am merely pointing out that the behaviors that can drive a parent mad can also provide a sense of comfort, normality and the feeling that all is right with the world. Did we teach Alex all those responsibilities? Of course we did. Had he forgotten everything he was taught? I hoped not. Actually, I knew that, deep down, Alex really had learned these lessons. He was just being a college kid. I knew the things we taught him would resurface at a later date, but it sure put things into perspective. Even as I reminded him to pick things up and turn things off, I had to smile at hearing the same old requests leaving my lips. And, as I would lie in my bed listening to Alex and his friends joking and debating until the wee hours of the morning, I relished the fact that he still enjoyed being home and having his friends over. There was a deep sense of satisfaction in knowing that there was still plenty of "kid" left in my tall, dark and handsome son.

Did I ever get annoyed? When the clock struck 3 a.m., or when there was a sudden rise in the charges on my electric bill, I could become a bit peeved. But then, before I knew it, the house would be quiet again, and I would once more be somewhat miserable, missing those "annoy-ing" moments. So, did I spend my time nagging, or did I just go with the flow and not waste our precious time together? I tended to use a lot of humor, with comments such as, "So *this* is what they are teaching you in college! Glad my money is going to a good cause!" It got the point across and we both got a good laugh.

For me, even now, summer with my child is a time to celebrate, but this is not so for all parents. As a child psychologist, I work with parents who tend to fall into one of two categories: The ones who are thrilled to have their kids home, and the ones who dread summer and can't wait for school to start again. For some, summer is a friend; for others it is a foe. Same event, different responses. Why? One word: Attitude!

Our attitude comes from the conscious and unconscious messages we send ourselves. These messages, or "self-talk," can be positive or nega-tive. Either way, they have a profound effect on our attitude, subsequent behavior, degree of enjoyment and, ultimately, the course of events. For example, if you are looking forward to taking your child to the zoo, your self-talk might go something like this: "I remember when my mom took me to the zoo. I always liked the giraffes best. It is great to share this experience with my son." If this is your self-talk, you will probably smile and be enthusiastic. As a result, your child will feel as though you really want to be with him or her, and you will probably both enjoy the day and each other's company.

On the other hand, your self-talk might say, "I have so much to do today; I wish I could get out of taking him to the zoo again. I really don't want to go in this heat. I hate the smell, and how many times does he need to see a giraffe, anyway?" As a result of these negative messages, you will probably be miserable and act impatiently, and your child will sense your annoyance, feel as though you don't want to be with him or her and perhaps, in return, will even act out in frustration.

Your attitude will determine the way you look at a situation. Are you an optimistic believer, or a pessimistic cynic? It's like the old question, "Is the glass half empty or half full?" A friend of mine once said that her mother always saw the glass as dirty. Now that's pessimism to the Nth degree! The pessimist tends to see the stress, difficulty and problems in life's situations. On the other hand, the optimist has a positive outlook on life, and views situations as opportunities for enjoyment, learning and accomplishment. It's all a matter of attitude. Basically, how you see life is how it is.

So, you can yell at your daughter for spilling her milk, you can tell your kids to "shut up" because they are too noisy, you can resent all the dirty clothes piled in the laundry room, you can spend the day giving your son the silent treatment to teach him a lesson—or not!

What about you? Do you cherish the little things, even as you correct, discipline and sometimes scold or yell? Can you put small matters into perspective and leave the annoyance for the really big issues? When you see your little girl with your lipstick all over her face, or your son with his new shoes covered in mud, is it really a time to yell and lose your temper? Or, are these the times to clean up, reprimand and secretly smile to yourself while filing the moment in your memory bank for heart-warming reflection at a later date?

Take it from someone who knows only too well. It's the little things that fill your home with the sweet presence of children, and these moments will be gone before you know it. When you don't have to deal with muddy shoes, "borrowed" lipstick and food wrappers anymore, will that really be a good thing?

Of all the people who help us grow, give us purpose and validate our best efforts, our children are the most important. Enjoy your time with them, and make summer a friend, not a foe.

 *Vicki F. Panaccione, Ph.D.*

PROTECT YOUR TEAM; PROTECT YOURSELF
Glenn W. Wooten, Sr.

I am a certified identity theft risk management specialist. In other words, I've been trained to inform you about the dangers and methods in which identity theft occurs. Despite what you think you know about the number one crime in the world, there's much more to it. The majority of media reports concentrate on financial or credit identity theft, but would you believe that credit identity theft comprises only 28 percent of all identity theft? The other 72 percent of cases are non-credit related. Why, then, is the focus on the financial realm? Because money touches every facet of our lives.

First, let's take a closer look at the five areas in which information is stolen in identity theft:

1. Character or criminal data
2. Credit/financial data
3. Department of Motor Vehicles data
4. Medical data
5. Social Security number

It can be devastating to have information stolen from any of these areas, and as it is the nation's No. 1 crime, it's not a matter of *if* it will happen, it's a matter of *when*. The numbers are staggering in America alone, showing more than 16,000 victims per day and growing. Would you believe that only one in 750 thieves are caught and prosecuted? So, whether you are a victim now or will be at some time in the future, you are going to need three things:

1. Access to qualified legal counsel in identity theft
2. Ongoing monitoring in all five areas
3. Professional identity restoration

As you can see, it will take an integrated team approach to address the legal, monitoring and restorative aspects of the problem. Having one part of the team without the others renders any attempt at total restoration incomplete and ineffective.

Many people think that correcting an identity theft problem is simple—until it happens to them. Just ask someone who has been arrested for mistaken identity or has written a check only to discover his account has been cleaned out by a thief. The statistics are alarming: A Gallup poll released in August 2005 found that roughly two-thirds of these people who had never been a victim of identity theft said they thought it was unlikely to happen to them. It's no wonder thieves find it so easy to turn people's lives upside down—too many people have the "it won't happen to me" mentality.

Most people have become complacent since identity theft doesn't require that the thief break into a home. All thieves have to do is wait until someone puts the trash out or places mail in a mailbox. In our high-tech society with private information floating around in cyberspace, thieves have access not only to you, but to everyone in your household, on your block and in your city with just one keystroke.

The average out-of-pocket expense incurred by identity theft victims was $500. For those who suffered from "New Accounts and Other Frauds" identity theft, the average monetary loss was $1,200.

The amount of time needed to correct identity theft issues depends largely upon how soon the theft is discovered. It's like a cancer: The sooner it's found, the easier it can be removed. The amount of time taken to correct identity theft ranges from one hour to more than 600 hours.

How would you like to spend your time and money taking care of a stolen identity? I can assure you it won't be easy or fun. How do you think your employer will respond when he or she discovers that you are spending all of your time at work trying to restore your identity? That's another problem. The majority of agencies that you will have to report your identity theft to are open only during normal working hours. Isn't that when you work, too? How will you get it done? Well, you can use only so many vacation days, sick days, lunch hours, etc. Do you get the picture? This is not the problem you want to take on by yourself.

Let's look at some common ways identity thieves might attack you. A low-tech method thieves used to steal identities is by stealing mail from your mailbox to look for account numbers, checks, personal information or even cash. Experts say consumers make it easy for thieves to steal mail by lifting the small red flag on their mailbox to alert the mail carrier that they have mail to be picked up also. This red flag alerts thieves as well.

Another way to lose information is to key your credit card number or password into a keypad or by giving it out over the telephone. The thief may be watching or listening over your shoulder, using a method called "shoulder surfing."

"Phishing" and "pharming" are two Web-based methods thieves use to steal information. Phishing is a scam that tricks people into giving out account numbers, their Social Security numbers, PIN numbers, passwords and other personal information via fake e-mails or fake Web site fill-in forms. These e-mails look as if they were sent from a company with whom the consumer has previously done business such as eBay, PayPal or banks and credit card companies.

Warning
Always look for these red flags to an identity phishing scam:
- Be cautious if a verification or a cancellation notice is sent via e-mail.
- Do not open the e-mail or fill in any information.
- Forward the questionable e-mail to spam@uce.gov.
- Call the company using the phone number from the company's official Web site, not the impostor site or e-mail.

- Look closely at the URL in the address bar at the top of your browser. Usually it will have a different domain name than the company it is pretending to be.
- Do not give any personal information to anyone who asks for it via the Internet or over the telephone.

"Pharming" is an electronic scam that targets personal information from many people at the same time via "domain spoofing." This consists of redirecting people to a fake Web site where hackers gather illegal information. The site will look very much like the real thing. The copycat pharming site mimics official bank Web sites and credit card Web sites so well that if you aren't paying attention, you will enter your personal information and soon discover that your account has been cleaned out.

"Skimming" is a very high-tech method in which thieves quickly steal credit card numbers and run them through an electronic reader that has been programmed to retrieve personal information. Your card only has to be out of your sight for mere minutes, such as when you give your card to a server at a restaurant. The thieves then harvest the card information later, either to make new clone cards or to simply use the information. Days later, thousands of dollars are charged and then the cloned cards are abandoned when the thieves move on to new victims.

Identity theft is real and very dangerous to your financial health. It is very important to use a team approach in protecting yourself and your identity.

Remember TEAM:

> Together
> Everyone
> Achieves
> More

Glenn W. Wooten, Sr.

TRANSFORMING FAMILY DYNAMICS
INTO A DYNAMIC FAMILY
Gayook, Jennifer and Matthew Wong

My mother's unexpected death came as a shock. We had spoken only two days before.

"You're not coming to see me, are you?" she asked.

"No, I can't afford to fly to New Jersey."

"I didn't think so," she replied.

Since my move to Hawaii, the conversation was always the same. I was overwhelmed with guilt that I wasn't with her. I wasn't the dutiful Chinese daughter. Shame engulfed me. The fact that I left home to heal from a life-threatening disease was little comfort.

When she died, the realization hit me with an almost physical force. The door had closed. I now had no hope of reconciliation.

I plummeted into a prolonged period of grief, something neither my children, Jennifer and Matthew, nor I expected. We'd been living and working in Hawaii for two years establishing a successful family business. As we were beginning to gel as a unit, everything fell apart!

My mother's death triggered memories of my troubled marriage. Once again, I suffered bouts of depression, rage and suicidal tendencies. I could barely function. I pushed my children away while becoming dependent upon them, never considering they, too, were grieving.

We had promised we would be there for each other, but now I had let my children down. Fearful of losing their mother, while resentful for having to assume my responsibilities, they shifted into automatic survival mode. They reverted to the time of the divorce, repeating those patterns of behavior.

What everyone thought was a cohesive family was, in reality, anything but. Things came to a head when I flew into a rage and grabbed the car keys. Jenn had to physically fight me for them. She was terrified I was going to kill myself. Only then did they finally speak up. I saw what I was doing to them—to our family. My behavior horrified me. I vowed that my children wouldn't go through with me what I went through with my mother!

Because of our fierce commitment to working things through, my children stuck by me until I struggled through my grief and regained my faith. We were determined to deal with any unresolved issues we had and came out stronger for it. Now, four years later, not only have we found each other, but we've discovered our mission in life—to teach organizations, families and individuals what we have learned.

We teach how group behavior is dictated by unconscious family dynamics. Families make us who we are. In our families, we learn positive and negative socialization skills. How we relate to each member of our family and our role within the family becomes the template for all future relationships, from friendship to marriage to work. In essence, we have successfully bridged the Eastern concepts of extended families and spirituality with the Western principles of independence and psychology.

Living and working together has been the most educational, frustrating and rewarding experience we've had. What we have accomplished together is far more powerful than anything achieved separately. We consciously work to maintain our individuality while still being an integral member of the group. We have created a loving and supportive environment where no one has to bear the weight of the world alone. We have someone who loves us unconditionally, without judgment.

And although we are far from perfect, we know that together we can overcome anything. And it wasn't until we helped each other work through our individual issues that we consciously transformed our family dynamics into a dynamic family!

 Gayook, Jennifer & Matthew Wong

MIRACLES OF LIGHT
DeNise McCarthy

M iracles manifest themselves in extraordinary ways. My life is a miracle; your life is miraculous, too.

For years, hope and faith have enabled all circumstances and situations to have favorable outcomes for me. The power of faith has lighted the way for me literally from blindness to sight. Being blind in one eye and knowing the comparison to sight makes you realize that complete vision is something not to be taken for granted. To be able to face each day with 20/20 vision and also a vision of the future is a gift. A motto of mine is, "Always envision positive outcomes." I have faced many challenges, including being unable to walk. Such life challenges are sometimes greater than we would like, but there is a greater power that is accessible for those who seek and ask. Through prayer, this power has had a new and greater meaning in my life.

Something is being offered to you each day. Choosing to embrace the positive is a matter of health. Accept positive influences; they illuminate your path. Hope is abundant and faith will be your guide.

Your walk of life will never be the same if you walk by faith and not by sight. Walking by faith is not contingent upon what is happening at that present moment. If someone were to ask exactly what was going to take place on a given day, you would have some idea of the schedule you would follow. When you are taken by surprise, this is called the "unexpected." So, it is not the event, but the initial expectation that causes the unexpected.

So, expect great things to happen and something good will happen. Be a magnet and draw the good into your life more and more. Faith is living constantly in the belief that something positive is going to happen, and whatever is happening in your life will be for the best.

These principles are applicable in all aspects of your life. If it is a career, then think about it, accept the fact that it is attainable, take action and believe. The same goes for health, relationships and any other area of your life: Health improvement, relationship improvement, career improvement, social improvement or self-improvement.

Once you have determined what you want to change:

- Design your life with lots of faith.
- Devote time until it becomes second nature.
- Determine that your outcome will be good.
- Dream with decisiveness and live it.

These factors can be implemented through an effort of collaborative teamwork—shifting from a focus on yourself to a focus on many individuals combined. It is virtually impossible to accomplish success solely on the basis of self. All areas of life are teamwork-oriented. In the career field, we make contacts and networks to take us where we want to go. Design your conversations with others with faith and positive thoughts; think that the outcome will be good. However the journey meanders, ultimately it will be a good one.

This is also applicable with health-related issues. If you focus on positive thoughts about your outcome, and partner with a good healthcare provider, you can produce significant results. A relationship is no different; it takes two. It then expands from two individuals to families and to others outside of that realm.

Years ago I had a small apartment. The space was inadequate and I wanted something larger. At the time, prices were a little high and finding a good apartment was a tedious task, but those factors didn't prevent me from pursuing my goal.

Without any knowledge of what the future held, I packed all of my belongings. As I continually searched for an apartment, I literally lived out of boxes. I didn't unpack anything because my mind and my actions had to correlate in order to bring results. Each day, as I looked at the boxes, I knew that something good was going to happen. I had gotten a phone call from a manager at a sought-after luxury building that I had visited. They had accommodations that exceeded my expectations. I was ecstatic. Everything happened very quickly, and soon I was in a much larger space, which was exactly what I had imagined.

When you have faith in something and combine it with action, it produces remarkable results. Many times this has been true in my life and has produced wondrous results. "As a man thinketh, so is he." It is never too late to start producing results.

All aspects of your life are like flowers; plant a good seed, then watch it prosper. If it is a business, it will grow. If it's your health, it will flourish. If it is a relationship or the path to righteousness, nurture it daily.

My car was starting to show some wear and tear and I wanted to get a new one. I didn't tell anyone at the time because the car I wanted was expensive. I thought and prayed about it and knew what I wanted. I envisioned the car and went shopping. I went to one dealership after another; some had cars close to what I wanted, but not really "the one." This went on for quite a while until one day I entered a dealership and could not believe my eyes—it was the car I had envisioned. The color and the interiors were exactly how I pictured them.

Faith has had a tremendous effect on my life. If visualization is not something that comes easily to you, then get a picture from a magazine or book that is a representation or similar to what you would like. Put this somewhere that is seen daily. This will be in your mind and soon you won't have to look at it to remember it. If you lack faith in your life, then ask through prayer and it will be increased.

On the road of life, if things seem to take an unexpected turn, don't fight it. This might be for your ultimate good. If you don't allow it, you may be your own hindrance. If we have it in our minds how things should happen, we tend to fight the circumstances. But this is not up to us. Knowledge of what you would like to happen is helpful, but just allow nature to take its course and you will see remarkable results. How many times have you said, "I didn't really plan that, it just happened?" Your frame of mind will attract these happy moments constantly if they are expected. Give yourself permission for wondrous things to happen in your life.

Allow the navigation system of your life to function on its own. Don't cause it to malfunction with indescribable thoughts or actions. Anything negative is defective. Cause it to function properly. Faith will take you further down the road than you can go without it.

Be an effective person with faith in your life—it's more powerful than you think.

 *DeNise McCarthy*

STOP FIGHTING AND LIVE THE LIFE YOU LOVE
Dr. David Trimble

O n one of the last few days of my grandmother's life, I asked her, if given the chance, what she would have done differently in her life. "Nothing," she replied. "Except Skippy's death." (Skippy was her son who had died young—he was hit by a car.) "It's so unnatural to have to bury your child," she added.

How strange—she wouldn't change anything? Her life seemed so uneventful, so empty of achievements. After all, I had spent my life racing to climb the ladder of success and achieve great things, and I could already put together a long list of things I would have changed.

My life seemed to have never-ending ebbs and flows, good times and bad, advances and set-backs; it was probably no different from anyone else's life, but it was always hard to understand: Why this? Why now? Why me? Yet, after each seemingly bad event, something great always followed. Sometimes it took a while, but the great thing always came. In fact, if you look at your life, I bet you will see the same pattern. I even reached a point when I decided I was the luckiest man alive. Then, just like that—why this? Why me? Why now?

Then a wonderful thing happened. Nearly unnoticeable events began to occur. I now recognize these events as a miraculous step-by-step learning process of how life really works, how we create our own lives and how we have the ability to re-create them. This understanding didn't come overnight—it took me years to understand and accept.

A long list of seminars, tapes and books began to slowly find their way into my life, often given to me by my wife, Cindy, or her sister, Darla. I often wondered why they were giving them to me, only to find myself totally engrossed.

Dr. Ted Morter's B.E.S.T. chiropractic technique began to open my eyes to the electromagnetic vibrations of the human body. Dr. Robert Becker's book, *The Body Electric*, gave research evidence. Kinesiology muscle testing gave me a working understanding of how energy vibrations can weaken or strengthen the human body. Then, a meeting with an incredible energy healer, Malcom Southwood, blew me away. All this led me to some of my favorite inspired authors—Neal Donald Walsh, Dr. Wayne Dyer, Lynn Grabhorn and Dr. David Hawkins, to name a few.

Through all of this, I have come to understand that the universe is full of various vibrational energy fields. Our thoughts, words and deeds create energy that connects with these vibrational fields and can ultimately create our world.

We are all blessed with the ability to create our world through the way in which we perceive it and interact with it. We can be in a traffic jam cursing the other drivers, the road construction and the feeling of being late, or we can concentrate on the fact that our car has air conditioning, that we have not been in an accident and that we have time to relax and think about the good in our day.

Our lives seem so full of negativity. The sad part is that we let them be this way. We do it to ourselves. What we watch on television, the news we read, music we listen to or gossip we hear all influence how we feel about life.

It comes down to this: Do you really want to live the life you love? If you do, then begin by loving the life you live. Find the positive; surround yourself with good and loving thoughts; look to your work, your family, your life. It is not easy to stay on the track of thinking about the good each and every day, but if you do, you will notice a change in how you feel. Those loving feelings create vibrations that connect with and are amplified by universal energy fields that change your life. Always remember that the joy in your life, your work and your family has nothing to do with function, and everything to do with purpose. You truly were born to live a glorious life.

I work each and every day to live this philosophy, and it is not always easy. I keep in mind my grandmother's perspective on her life. I remember the wisdom passed on to me by my family members—members of my team. I try not to fight life so hard and I have been able to find more things in my life I love. And, you know, my life really has been wonderful.

So, each day, love the life you live. Don't be afraid to listen to the advice of your trusted team members, family, friends and even inspired authors. Even though you may not notice it sneaking up on you, your life will unfold and you will soon be living the life you love.

 *Dr. David Trimble*

UNLEASH THE GREATNESS WITHIN
Dan Lok

This is a story about a little boy named Danny. He immigrated to North America when he was 13 years old. Even though he couldn't speak or write a word of English, his parents put him in a school where everyone else could. Because he couldn't communicate with the other students, Danny couldn't express himself. He didn't speak much, and he didn't really have any friends.

Other students thought he was weird. They weren't very kind and they constantly made fun of him. He was even beaten up a few times by bullies.

The poor little guy would always sit in the back of the classroom by himself. He never put his hand up for questions, because he really didn't understand what the teacher was saying. Danny was afraid he would embarrass himself because of the way he spoke. He didn't want to be a laughing stock to his classmates, so he suffered in silence.

Every day after school, Danny would race back home and lock himself in his room and watch TV alone. Can you blame him? Can you imagine going to a foreign country where you couldn't speak or write the language? How could you possibly make friends or expect to do well in school?

As time went on, Danny became more and more depressed. He completely lost his self-esteem. In fact, he felt so bad about himself that he constantly stared at the ground when he was walking, and he never looked anyone in the eye when he spoke with them.

Because of his poor English skills, Danny was barely passing any of his subjects in school. One day, Danny actually failed one of his geography exams. His teacher was disgusted with him and said, "Do you know that you got the lowest score on this exam? I've never had a student as stupid as you." But the teacher didn't stop there! He said, "If you keep this up, you'll never be able to graduate from high school."

Poor Danny didn't know what to say. He just stood there and started to cry, which just made things worse. The geography teacher looked at this kid with tears running down his cheeks and told him, "You're hopeless—nothing but a crybaby! I don't even want to look at you. You'll never amount to anything. Get out of my office!"

That little boy's heart was crushed. He went home, locked himself in his room and cried. He thought to himself, "I hate school. I hate my parents. I hate my instructors. I hate everyone. Maybe that teacher is right: I am stupid; I am a loser."

As if that humiliation wasn't enough, one day, Danny found out he was going to have to do a three-minute oral presentation in front of his entire English class. He was absolutely terrified. He couldn't sleep, he couldn't eat and he couldn't think about anything except how scared he was.

Finally, even though he was scared and embarrassed, he approached his English teacher, Miss Fallon. He said to her, "Miss Fallon, I don't want to do my presentation. I am afraid." Fortunately, Miss Fallon knew something about children and something about teaching. Instead of yelling at him, she just asked him, "What seems to be the problem?"

"I just can't do it," Danny said. "I just can't do it. People will laugh at me."

She didn't make fun of his fears. She listened to his concerns. "Nobody's going to laugh at you," she told him. "If they do, I'll punish them. Remember, in order to graduate from this class, you have to do the presentation. It's one of the requirements."

Miss Fallon then put her hand on Danny's shoulder. "There's still a week's time before the presentation," she said. "Why don't you come to my office after school? You can practice and I'll be your audience. Okay?" Danny thought about it for a moment and finally agreed. For the first time in a long time, he thought that things might actually be okay.

Finally, the big day arrived. Danny was scheduled to give his three-minute speech to the class. He was nervous, but he had been practicing with Miss Fallon for a whole week.

Danny's heart was pounding. His palms were sweaty. He felt like he was going to throw up or pass out. He suddenly understood what grown-ups meant when he'd heard them say, "I'd rather die than speak in public."

Danny had a lot of self-doubt, but he had something else, too. He had a promise that he'd made to himself. After all she'd done for him, he didn't want to disappoint Miss Fallon. And he didn't! His presentation went smoothly from start to finish. When it was all over, Danny said to himself, "They didn't laugh at me. They didn't make fun of me. People actually gave me some applause! Wow!"

It was only a three-minute speech, but for Danny, it was a declaration of independence. It boosted his self-esteem and shot his confidence through the roof!

That speech was a turning point for Danny; it was a wake-up call. Miss Fallon was the person who helped make it happen. She had been the boy's mentor and she completely changed his life in the most positive way.

Slowly, Danny began to have a better understanding of the English language and, as his English improved, his grades also improved. He successfully graduated from high school and went to college.

He even joined the Toastmasters organization so he could conquer that grown-up fear he knew about—public speaking. With his new confidence and drive, Danny was able to complete the Competent Toastmaster course in just two-and-a-half months, when most people spend from six to 10 months on it.

To no one's surprise, Danny was elected president of his Toastmasters club. He became the youngest person in his province to hold the office. Under his leadership, the club received the prestigious "President Distinguished" award from Toastmasters International that year.

The little boy who spoke very little English is now a best-selling author. The boy has become a man who has achieved financial freedom, is a highly respected entrepreneur and whose work is read and studied by hundreds of thousands of people.

He now mentors others like him to help them find their greatness in the same way he found his.

The little boy who once almost threw up because he had to give a three-minute speech to his English class is now a man able to speak to hundreds, or even thousands, of people and hold them in the palm of his hand without breaking a sweat.

When he was standing in front of that English class, Danny could never have imagined in his wildest dreams that he would someday speak and write for a living. And to be honest, if it wasn't for Miss Fallon, he wouldn't have.

Without Miss Fallon as a mentor and without her there to recognize the little boy's talents and unleash that greatness within him, it's pretty clear that his life would have turned out differently—maybe even tragically.

He and Miss Fallon made a great team.

I know beyond question that this story is true. The little boy doesn't use the name "Danny" anymore; I prefer "Dan."

 Dan Lok

EMBRACE SILENCE
Dr. Wayne Dyer

You live in a noisy world, constantly bombarded with loud music, sirens, construction equipment, jet airplanes, rumbling trucks, leaf blowers, lawn mowers and tree cutters. These manmade, unnatural sounds invade your senses and keep silence at bay.

In fact, you've been raised in a culture that not only eschews silence, but is terrified of it. The car radio must always be on, and any pause in conversation is a moment of embarrassment that most people quickly fill with chatter. For many, being alone in silence is pure torture.

The famous scientist Blaise Pascal observed, "All man's miseries derive from not being able to sit quietly in a room alone."

With practice, you can become aware that there's a momentary silence in the space between your thoughts. In this silent space, you'll find the peace that you crave in your daily life. You'll never know that peace if you don't have any spaces between your thoughts.

The average person is said to have 60,000 separate thoughts a day. With so many thoughts, there are almost no gaps. If you could reduce that number by half, you would open up an entire world of possibilities for yourself. For it is when you merge into the silence, and become one with it, that you reconnect to your source and know the peacefulness that some call "God." It is stated beautifully in Psalms of the Old Testament: "Be still and know that I am God." The key words are "still" and "know."

"Still" actually means "silence." Mother Teresa described silence and its relationship to God by saying, "God is the friend of silence. See how nature (trees, grass) grows in silence. We need silence to be able to touch souls." This includes your soul.

It's really the space between the notes that make the music you enjoy so much. Without the spaces, all you would have is one continuous, noisy note. Everything that's created comes out of silence. Your thoughts emerge from the nothingness of silence. Your words come out of this void. Your very essence emerged from emptiness.

All creativity requires some stillness. Your sense of inner peace depends on spending some of your life energy in silence to recharge your batteries, removing tension and anxiety, thus reacquainting you with the joy of knowing God and feeling closer to all of humanity. Silence reduces fatigue and allows you to experience your own creative juices.

The second word in the Old Testament observation, "know," refers to making your personal and conscious contact with God. To know God is to banish doubt and become independent of others' definitions and descriptions of God. Instead, you have your own personal knowing. And, as Melville reminded us so poignantly, "God's one and only voice is silence."

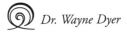 *Dr. Wayne Dyer*

INNER CIVIL WAR
Johnny Morney

Our mind can be the No. 1 enemy to our success. The ruler of the Kingdom of Failure knows that if he or she can manipulate how we think, then they will be able to manipulate our lives.

When you are on a team, not only does the enemy target your mind, but he also targets the vision or mission of the team. If the adversary can sway and direct the team's belief in the mission, then he can influence the outcome of projects and goals. Thoughts determine our actions, attitudes and destinies. Our lives will always follow our thoughts.

You and your team will never go beyond the barriers of your own minds. If you think you can't do something, then you never will. If the team is defeated in its thoughts, then the battle has already been lost.

I worked with the U.S. Military and Coalition Forces in Iraq during Operation Iraqi Freedom. We worked with the Iraqi people to help restore their country to a position of prominence. This is where I really learned the importance of teamwork and cooperation in achieving a common goal. We had to take the teamwork concept to another level because working together meant more than whether or not we completed a project on time, below cost or ahead of schedule. Our cooperation was crucial because it might mean the difference between life and death, so we had to put our individual differences aside and work as one unit with one mission.

I want to issue an alert—read very carefully. You and your team members may not be in Iraq or in the military, but rest assured, you *are* in a war. You are under attack as an individual, and so is the rest of your team. I also want to report that one of the greatest battles you or your team will ever fight in your life is between your ears. Your mind is a battlefield—I call the battle of the mind "inner civil war:" The struggle between good and bad, right and wrong, prosperity and poverty, abundance and scarcity, success and failure. I will be so bold as to say you are probably at inner civil war right now. Your heart and mind are possibly clashing over whether or not you are worthy of your goals, or maybe your team can't come to a consensus on a major project.

In order to win this battle, you should associate with successful people who believe *it can be done* and who constantly look for ways to accomplish your goals. This way, you will continue to condition yourself for success. In the heat of battle, a team's primary objective should be to immerse each other in a positively-charged environment in which everyone focuses on positive thoughts, positive ideas and positive action.

We did some great work in Iraq because we firmly believed anything was possible. There is absolutely nothing in the world that you and your team cannot accomplish with a "can do" attitude. My team needed optimistic members who could find the metaphorical silver lining in the cloud, not only to give each other a ray of hope, but to give hope to the Iraqi people as well. In certain situations, we all felt desperate. That's why you need winners on your team to keep you focused and to take you to the next level of achievement. To win the inner civil war, you must hang around incredible people who pump you up instead of bringing you down.

You'll be surprised to see the great things that can be accomplished when a group's unlimited positive thinking comes together. It is exhilarating to feel the enthusiasm and energy a group of positively-charged champions can produce. Ross Perot said, "When building a team, I always search first for people who love to win. If I can't find any of those, I look for people who hate to lose."

As a champion, you must create the "can do" attitude by defeating the negative thoughts that surface during your inner civil war. The mind seems to have a never-ending arsenal of negativity to shoot down our goals.

Champions are attracted to other champions. That means you should surround yourself with a winning combination of self-starters and positively-charged players. You need to make certain that you demonstrate the traits of a champion in order to attract champions, not chumps.

I can tell you all about the ensuing disaster that accompanies the loss of an inner civil war. You see, I have personally experienced the ruins that usually follow the loss of such a skirmish. At one such time, my life was reduced to rubble, not by the enemies from the outside, but by the enemy within—me.

When I was on drugs, my life was one battle after another. I looked perfectly fine from the outside, but on the inside, rockets were blowing up and car bombs were exploding. It took years before I understood that I didn't lose the battle when I went to the drug house, I lost the battle when I allowed the thought of going to the drug house dwell in my mind.

Similarly, you don't lose the battle when you eat that piece of cake after swearing this time you would stick to your diet. You don't lose the battle when you purchase those cigarettes after promising never to smoke again. You lose the battle when you entertain defeatist thoughts in your mind. You lose when you allow yourself to be bombarded with negative thoughts until you are defeated. When this happens, you are waving the white flag and surrendering.

I know what it feels like to be under enemy control. Many of these times, I was my own worst enemy. It is crucial for you to understand that your dreams will not be given to you on a silver platter. The fears, obstacles and challenges you are working to overcome will not go away without a fight. My friend, you are at war.

When I was in inner civil war, I was torn between my heart's desire and my outer situation—which seemed to be hopeless. Given the fact that I focused most of my energy on my past mistakes and failures, I allowed the enemy to convince me that I was supposed to lose the war. After all, I was a victim of my past.

I became a POW, and I don't mean a prisoner of war—I was a "prisoner of words"—the negative, disempowering, self-defeating words others spoke to me. Even more demoralizing were the negative words I spoke to myself. I tormented and beat myself with negative words of self-defeat, self-abuse, self-judgment, guilt and regret. What do you do when the enemy comes from within? You must recognize that you could be the biggest hindrance preventing yourself from living the life of which you dream.

I must tell you that it can be frightening to realize you are the traitor that has given terrorists the top-secret information that has been used to sabotage your own dreams. What valuable information are you and your team giving these enemies?

Now that you recognize that you and your team are at war, it's time to develop your winning battle plan. This is a war you must win.

 *Johnny Morney*

MOVE HIM UP!
Gene Brugger

The capacity crowd was chanting, "Move him up! Move him up!" I was turning three shades of crimson at center ice. This was supposed to be a relaxing evening of fun. The crowd was having a great time, but it was at my expense. How did this happen and what the heck am I doing here?

We were at my in-law's home on Thanksgiving afternoon when my wife's Uncle Howie and his wife stopped in. Now, Uncle Howie is a real piece of work, and one of the most rabid sports fans I've ever known. Howie doesn't live in Detroit, but he's a major Detroit fan. One Sunday morning he called to me across the church (between services) saying, "Gene! He's got'em going! He's really got'em going!" referring to the Tigers' manager at the time.

I was not surprised by his excitement, I expected it; excitement seemed to be his normal state. But that Sunday I assumed he would boast about the arrival of his new grandson born that week, or congratulate me on the birth of our new baby girl.

He was excited about the Tigers. During the afternoon that Thanksgiving, Howie mentioned he was thinking of attending a hockey game that evening. He said he'd give me a call if I'd be interested in going. He did, and we met at the game.

I passed on buying a program when we entered, but after the first period I needed definitions for the hockey terms I didn't understand, so I went and bought one. Returning to my seat, I heard the announcer advise everyone to check their programs for a certain number. Shockingly I had the number!

As I walked down to the announcer's booth, I thought about the time my ticket was drawn for the door prize at a PTA meeting. That teapot was the only thing I could remember ever winning. As a second grade boy, I had made the long walk back from the front of the auditorium carrying what I thought was the most ridiculous prize ever. I feared school the next day, fervently hoping that none of my classmates would find out that I'd won a teapot the night before.

Now, rather than handing me the teapot I expected, the guy took my name and directed me to the penalty box. A bit confused, I stepped into the box and asked the boy, who was probably eight or nine, and the older gentleman already in the penalty box what this was all about.

The boy said incredulously, "Don't you know? It's the 'shoot the puck' contest!"

He was excited, and I seriously considered bolting. While I knew nothing about shooting a puck, I did know that I stood an excellent chance of landing on my back side.

I reluctantly decided to stay, they would soon be announcing my name, and I couldn't have them doing that and no one responding.

They placed a board over the net with a small opening in the middle.

Sizing up my competition in the contest, I asked the boy if he played hockey a lot. I felt my stomach tighten when he said, "Oh, yeah, all the time."

The holiday crowd was really into the festivities and cheered loudly as the boy was announced and strode confidently to center ice. He sent his first shot on its way, but it slowed and stopped short of the goal.

Not missing a beat, the crowd began to chant, "Move him up!" The officials responded by moving him halfway to the goal.

All too soon, the announcer blared my name and I stepped onto the ice.

I remember thinking I must have resembled a woman's first walk in five inch heels.

The official smiled kindly. He had several sticks to choose from and seemed to appreciate my predicament when I told him that it didn't matter.

I had no idea of how hard I needed to hit the puck, and it showed as my first shot slid to a stop short of the goal, just as the boy's had. And just as they did with the boy, they immediately began to chant, "Move him up!"

They were joking, since everyone knew they wouldn't afford the same consideration to a 30 year old adult as they did the boy. They were just having fun . . . having lots of fun at my expense.

I was embarrassed.

I did not know if my second shot would find the net, but I knew that it would definitely reach that board!

I sent the second puck on its way with an authority that had been lacking in my first shot. It slammed into the edge of the right side of the opening and went in.

You would have thought it was a real home team goal by the way the crowd erupted into a deafening roar. They were still having fun and, even though I knew their cheer was a bit facetious, it felt better than their derisive chant of "Move him up!"

Relieved now, I just wanted off the ice as quickly as possible. I slapped my final shot toward the goal with more than sufficient steam and it banged into the board. At that point I didn't care. I'd made one, won some nice prizes and, except for my return walk across the ice, it was over.

My hockey story has served me well since then. It helps break the ice when I'm chatting with folks I've just met. A little self deprecating humor works well in a lot of settings.

But over time I've come to understand that my heavenly Father is more deeply concerned with me than I ever imagined; that He extends His favor toward me in a myriad of ways. I now know that He is for me and not the ogre I heard about as a kid. In fact, my heavenly Father provides me with the unconditional love we all search for. I like to picture Him leaning over the banister of Heaven and admonishing the angels that Psalm 91 says are around to help me to, "Move him up!"

 *Gene Brugger*

A PASSION FOR GIVING: THE ANTHONY ROBBINS FOUNDATION
Anthony Robbins

Global Impact
The Anthony Robbins Foundation was created in 1991 with the belief system that, regardless of stature, only those who have learned the power of sincere and selfless contribution experience life's deepest joy: true fulfillment. The Foundation's global impact is provided through an international coalition of caring donors and volunteers who are connecting, inspiring and providing true leadership throughout the world!

Global Relief Efforts
The Anthony Robbins Foundation offers its heartfelt compassion to the victims of the numerous natural disasters felt throughout the world. The Foundation is passionate about participating in the coordination of reconstruction activities and evaluates funding requests on an ongoing basis. As men and women affected by these disasters begin to rebuild, the Anthony Robbins Foundation takes honor in providing hope and funding support to the many suffering communities.

Adopt-A-School Program, New Orleans, USA
Katrina Relief Efforts continue to be a focus of the Foundation. The Foundation will support the rebuilding efforts throughout the Gulf Coast through a partnership with its Youth Mentoring Program partner, Communities In Schools (CIS). CIS is the nation's leading community-based stay-in-school network, connecting needed community resources with schools. CIS has over 34 chapters serving well over 2 million children nationally. The Foundation will focus on rebuilding the educational infrastructure currently affecting thousands of children in Louisiana, Mississippi, and Alabama.

The Foundation is proud to announce its partnership with the Adopt-A-School Program in New Orleans to support the rebuilding efforts of

Ben Franklin Elementary. This elementary school was the first public school to open in New Orleans post-Katrina. Ben Franklin Elementary is operating near its capacity by serving 555 students, a 24% increase in student population since Hurricane Katrina. Over 90% of its students reside in high poverty households. The Foundation will provide funding and hands-on assistance toward rebuilding the library, playground and other structural needs. The Foundation's goal is to provide the funds and tools necessary to transform this elementary school into an enhanced learning environment.

Adopt-A-School Program, The Citizens Foundation, Pakistan
The Anthony Robbins Foundation will provide support to The Citizens Foundation which manages many relief programs in Pakistan, rebuilding schools and homes following the earthquake on October 8, 2005. It is widely recognized that, because of crumbling schools, the children suffered the greatest blow from the October quake. It has been reported that some 10,000 schools collapsed throughout Pakistan. The Anthony Robbins Foundation is proud to support the construction of a 6,500 square foot school in the Bagh district of Kashmir, Pakistan. Upon completion, this school will serve 180 students during the academic year beginning in April 2007.

Hebron Orphanage, India
Over the past 40 years, Hebron Orphanage has saved homeless orphans from dying of starvation on the streets of southern India. These orphaned children have been given love, life and a future. The Anthony Robbins Foundation adopted Hebron Orphanage following the 2004 Tsunami. The orphanage has expanded its facilities and now accommodates 400 children. The Foundation is delighted to provide funding to support Hebron Orphanage's immediate need to build a new standalone boy's dormitory, enabling the number of male residents to increase to 100, and to allow the current boy's dormitory to be used as a library and classrooms.

Langfang Children's Village, Beijing China
The Langfang Children's Village in Beijing, China was founded to support mainland China's orphaned and special needs children. Many children come to the village because they are abandoned at the front gates or brought to the Langfang by locals. It is home to more than 90 orphans from approximately 10 different orphanages scattered throughout China. China is working hard at improving the plight of these children, but as a developing country with over 5 million orphans, the problem is simply too large.

The Langfang Children's Village is designed to model a normal family environment and de-emphasizes the institutional feel often associated with orphanages. Every child lives in a freestanding home with house parents and their own yard to play in. The Anthony Robbins Foundation provides funding to the Langfang Children's Village to support the daily needs of the children as well as medical treatment at an on-location clinic. This collaborative effort is contributing to the well-being of these beautiful children, allowing the Foundation to work toward fulfilling its mission of global impact.

Global Community Connection Day
The Anthony Robbins Foundation proudly sets aside one day a month to proactively connect with non-profit organizations throughout the world. Its goal is to meet the challenges of a global community, come up with solutions and TAKE ACTION! We visit and provide in-kind donations to schools, hospitals, and shelters for the homeless to nurture, feed and mentor those in need. Recently, the Foundation supported the Children's Hospitals of San Diego and New Orleans with donations of stuffed bears for their in-patients. The Foundation also supported the Diabetes Association in their annual Tour de Cure cycling event held in San Diego and Santa Monica, California in honor of the National Physical Fitness and Sports Month.

Anthony Robbins

THE GREATEST TEAM OF ALL
Sharon Worsley

Now that I am in my 40s, I look back at my life and notice all the people who have been part of my "team." The list includes teachers, trainers, employers, friends, mentors, fellow employees, family members and even good books written by enlightened authors.

They have all been contributors to my success as a professional and who I have become as a person in the world. Some know the impact they have had on my life, and others passed through so quickly that even I wasn't fully aware of their influence until they had stepped from my path. Either way, each of them taught me life lessons that have been indelibly inked into my DNA.

My closest team members were my parents. They had a vision for a better life for their family, so they sold their home and business in Montreal and packed up their two children to move to Sydney, Australia, in 1970. They believed that starting a new life in what was still a rather unknown country in the 70s offered their children the best chance for a great future.

My parents—especially my father—were my biggest cheerleaders. In my late teens and early 20s, I wanted to work in the travel industry. At the time, it was hard to break into this field, but I pursued it with great fervor by working a full-time job and going to school two to four nights per week for several years. My father would wait for me each evening until class was over. He parked his car near the school and took a nap until 9 p.m.

While at school, I decided that if I was going to work in travel I needed some hands-on experience. So I negotiated for a position at a branch of a large travel agency every Thursday night for free. This meant an additional night my father waited in the car for me to finish. He never complained, but instead felt that this was a great gift he could give to his daughter.

Once I was hired by Ansett Airlines I set my sights on the bigger goal: To work for Qantas Airways in their International Travel Center in downtown Sydney. At the time, it was very difficult to obtain such a position without spending a year or so in the reservations department, but I was not deterred in my quest. This just meant that once I had won my goal, the payoff would be even sweeter.

I still remember that day in 1986, driving home with my dad along the Hume Highway, celebrating the victory: I was hired by Qantas. We stuck our heads out of the car windows, screaming at the top of our lungs!

In 1988, I made the decision to move from Sydney to Toronto to sell travel to the South Pacific. It was a joyful, yet painful, decision, as I realized that I would no longer be able to be with my family on a daily basis. In the beginning, I struggled to make ends meet, but my parents—my team—continued to help me with my bills so I could fulfill my dream of living in Canada.

After losing my mother to a stroke, I received a call just before Christmas in 1996 from my father saying that he had terminal cancer. My whole world was shaken as I again had to come to terms with the loss of someone I cared about so deeply.

I traveled to Sydney for an unexpected visit that Christmas. My father, brother and I went to visit the site of my brother's future home, which was still under construction. I still remember standing in front of the site, hearing my father tell both of us that even though he and my mom had never made a great deal of money in their lives, it was comforting for him to know that at least when he was gone, he would be able to give us both a little savings toward our first homes. Six weeks later, I rushed back to Sydney. I wanted to be at his bedside when he went to be with my mother.

In December 2004, I finally moved into my little condominium in Toronto with a sad and heavy heart. I was thrilled to finally have my own home but I didn't have my faithful team member—who, during his life, acted more like my fan club president—walking in the door with me. Without my father in my life, I have had to look elsewhere for team members to support me. I have found some in friends, church members and even strangers.

I have come to realize that it is important to consider and recognize who is on your team. Are they looking out for your best interests by watching your back? Are they prepared to ask you the tough questions when no one else will, so as to support your continued progress? When times get tough, will your "team" stand behind you, or will they disappear when things get uncomfortable?

Experts say that we are the product of the five or 10 people with whom we surround ourselves. If that is even partially true, then what does that say about you and your success in life? What does that say about your team members?

Conversely, what does that say about you as a team member in someone else's life? Are you worthy to be there supporting them? If you expect the best from *your* team, how are you showing up as a team member for someone else? Not only are we supported by a team, we are a part of a team of support for those around us.

Teamwork is really "life."

 *Sharon Worsley*

LIVE YOUR DREAM
Debbie Wysocki

We all have dreams—or at least we start out that way. Some people end up putting theirs on a shelf when they grow up, but if you're reading this, I'm guessing that's not you!

My dreams started when I was a little girl, and my biggest dream was to be a wife and mother. I'm happy to say that this dream finally came true, and more. You see, during all those years I dreamed about being a wife and mother, I had a certain vision on the kind of life I wanted. Of course, we get glimpses of fairy tale lives on television, but when I was about 20, I got a preview of a lifestyle I knew was destined for me; it was a glimpse into the world of network marketing.

Like most 20-year-olds, I had a few detours along the way. I wanted an exciting corporate career, and I was blessed to start off in a high-level position as assistant to the CEO of The Times-Mirror Company, but I soon hit the glass ceiling. Then I went on to become a Beverly Hills financial analyst for 11 years. This required 60- to 90-hour work weeks, plus substantial commuting.

One day I woke up and realized I was like a hamster on a never-ending wheel, and I didn't know how to get off. This definitely looked like the dream life—I had all the trappings of success, a six-figure income, sports car, beautiful home, flights on private jets and front row seats to sporting events. My career even led me to meet my husband. But something was missing.

Well, God has a plan for all of us. Shortly after my beautiful oceanfront wedding in 1994, when I should have been on top of the world, I was stricken with a symphony of symptoms: depression, hair loss, loss of strength and incredible pain throughout my body. I literally thought I was dying at the age of 33. The diagnosis was fibromyalgia. The treatment wasn't pretty—a handful of prescription drugs, each pill caus-ing another symptom. And to make matters worse, in the middle of this diagnosis, we moved across the country to Florida. Still trying to keep my boss happy, I was bi-coastal, working one week in California, one week in Florida. It was a recipe for disaster.

About this time, a friend shared a business idea, the concept I had actu-ally seen 14 years earlier at the age of 20. Only now, I was ready to move—I was open to change.

In just two-and-a-half years I was able to replace my six-figure income and create a lifestyle that today allows me to live a life few people get to enjoy. Through network marketing, I learned how to leverage the abili-ties of other people and use the power of a network, or team, to reach my goals.

Now we live a hop, skip and a jump from the beach in Fort Lauderdale, Florida, in a beautiful home where my custom-built office overlooks a spectacular pool and wonderful entertainment area. I wake when I am rested, work a few hours each day and get to be the kind of mother I always knew I would be. We vacation six to eight weeks a year, and more importantly, we are changing lives by teaching others how to live their dreams.

When our children, Trent and Amanda, came along, I got to enjoy every minute instead of sending them off to daycare. Now I get to be the "Room Mom," "Craft Mom" and "Cookie Mom" at my kids' school. I am creating memories hands-on. If the school calls me, I don't have to ask a boss if I can leave early; I am right there.

I can't imagine what my life would be without this business. If I hadn't listened to my friend, I might be back in a stressful job, leaving my kids in daycare and working to make someone else's dreams a reality, proba-bly at a cost to my health and perhaps personal relationships. No time for freedom.

My family is my best support team. My husband, Mark, is a partner in a real estate law firm and loves his job. Still, we know that his job has limited flexibility. He has been incredibly supportive of me building a strong team because of the financial freedom. Our children have learned about the benefits of working for yourself. They have learned to be generous, to be encouragers, negotiators and team players. They have learned flexibility and the importance of good marketing. These are life skills that could benefit many adults.

Our children have experienced personal development firsthand, and they see me building teams of winning people. They know about the power of dream boards, affirmations and attitude. Our mantra is, "Think you can, think you can't—either way, you're right." The kids are great at sharing the business, too. Both of them are good at asking questions and getting phone numbers. I can only imagine what they will accomplish as adults.

The teams behind my two organizations, *Women with Dreams* and *Residual Money Secrets*, have impacted thousands of lives, and it all started with a dream to create freedom for me and to create change for others. My family has seen what being true to your dream can mean and how it can really mean big changes for people. You have no glass ceiling and no limits when you take action to live your dream.

I now know that, "If you want things you've never had before, you've got to do things you've never done before."

 *Debbie Wysocki*

SERVE OTHERS; BUILD A TEAM
Larry Benet

Who are the most successful business men or women you know; the ones you most respect? For me, it is Oprah Winfrey, Richard Branson and Bill Gates. What do they all have in common? Some might say they are billionaires, and they would be right. Some might say they have extensive impact and influence millions of people because of their products, services and personalities. Some might say they inspire fierce loyalty from their employees, colleagues and business partners.

But if you look closer, their common quality is that they have discovered success through the support of others. They have built powerful teams to help them get things done. What is the core of all this ambition? What is the glue that holds it all together? It is the relationships they have with people. Oprah, Branson and Gates are all very rich, but the reason for their success is that they have rich relationships with people, built on the desire to help others.

If you want to build a loyal team:
Focus on WE not I
Focus on giving back to others
Focus on serving others
Focus on adding value to others
Focus on following up over long periods of time
And then, after people know how much you care, they can see how you can work together to accomplish mutually beneficial goals.

If you want to figure out how well you are doing, you can look at your results. Do you have a lot of people willing to follow you? Do you have "contacts" or are they connections?

This is an important distinction. Those to whom you are connected are linked to you by more than acquaintance. You share a common interest, belief or—most important—goal. Have you ever noticed if you can motivate people for long periods of time? They have to be self-motivated. If you are helping someone accomplish what is most important to them, as long as it ties in to your initiatives, the results will be beneficial for everyone. I think you will find that "one plus one equals eleven," as my mentor Mark Victor Hansen likes to say.

There is one last piece of advice I will share with you. If you are reading this and say to yourself, "Well, I know all this already," ask yourself if you are implementing what you know. Common knowledge isn't always commonly practiced.

When you have challenges, ask yourself, "What would Oprah do in this situation? What would Richard Branson do in this situation? What would Bill Gates do in this situation? Am I focusing on serving others or am I focused on serving my own interests?" Are you building relationships, or are you just building contacts?

By applying these simple ideas, you will undoubtedly achieve more by building a powerful team. The power of team is unstoppable.

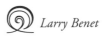 *Larry Benet*

WHAT AN AWESOME TIME IT IS TO BE ALIVE!
Janet Florence McCormack

The soft cooing of a morning dove serenades me as I sit at my laptop. My knees press comfortably on the padding of an ergonomic back chair and my bare feet touch the cool tiles of stone flooring. The bright southeastern Arizona sunlight shines into my room, rising in a clear, blue sky above rich, riparian bosque along the Santa Cruz River. I am filled with gratitude to be graced with the privilege of life on this planet today.

I've already done my morning meditation, joining others around the globe in an experiment of peace building. More than six billion human beings populate the Earth today. Technologies like the Internet speed our thoughts to one another, surrounding this celestial orb with our imaginings. It's a dynamic world, alive with billions of beings manifesting reality in a holographic soup of energy! For some, this is indeed a new age, never before experienced in traditional human history. For others, this is only another turning in the cosmic cycle of life.

For me, it is a time of joy and exploration. Awakened to new understandings about how this world operates, I wholeheartedly accept my responsibility as one of the meaning-makers today. I am no longer willing to be stuck in a consciousness of victimization, blaming and complaining. My life is mine to manage; how well I do that affects everyone else today. Call it the "butterfly effect" or any other name—I know I am not alone. I am connected to everything and everyone by an invisible flow of energy.

Like everyone, I make millions of choices from moment to moment. Some are made automatically from deep in my subconscious, and others come from the twisting and turning of thoughts in my head. I am a babbling baby boomer, enjoying a journey of freedom in a land of luxurious liberty. I am grateful to be alive at this awesome time of rapid change.

I find all of these changes stimulating, because change is an essential part of learning and growth. I love learning! Since early childhood I've felt called to teach, minister and lead others to discover their own inner gifts and power. Yes, I've bungled that effort many times. I've acted too quickly or expressed irritation when life didn't match my expectations, but now I catch myself much sooner. I am more aware of the discomfort I feel when my inner peace has waned. Before I express my confusion, I slow down, breathe deeply and center myself, going within to that place of connection, to the ancient wisdom available to all. In only a few moments, I return my being to that miraculous state of harmony and strength. It has taken me 60 years to learn to do this. Blessed with many mentors and models to show me the way, I join the throngs of millions who are making a similar journey these days.

My external circumstances will change. When I have doubts about the future and how the rest of my life may unfold, I take charge, reach out and exert the due diligence required to direct my life. How I experience this life, how I use my gifts, how I overcome obstacles, how I process pain and pleasure, how I respond to and interact with others and how I live is my choice and my responsibility. The consequences, results and outcomes belong to me and my ability to live through a filter of empathy and love. The design of the universe holds each of us accountable for how our choices affect others.

Healthy, heartfelt laughter at silly things soothes symptoms of the syndrome of seriousness. Engaging forgiveness for any sour notes, shrillness or dissonance, I make music with each beat of my heart. Striving to listen better, hearing the silence between the notes and attending to the sounds and sensations of others, I play on. I honor the signals to rest, savoring moments of reflection, seeking guidance from beyond. Rejoicing in the harmonies and melodies we make together, I am in concert with billions of other beings; I am only one of the many.

And you—a beloved being receiving these words—you are one of those billions, too. Play your part with furious curiosity and joyful discovery. This is indeed an awesome symphony we play!

 *Janet Florence McCormack*

UNITED WE STAND, DIVIDED WE FALL
Oliver Nims

The opportunity is upon us to create a new culture of peace.

The culture of war, as old as humanity itself, has come to a head. It is no longer an acceptable way to resolve conflict. The culture of war is sustained by greed, anger and stupidity, and is also one of reaction; focusing on the effects rather than the cause. It is as effective as trying to lose weight by drinking diet soda, or paying bills with your credit cards. Silly! The culture of war is full of customs like violence, defense, power struggle, revenge and escalation.

Let's look at another possibility—the culture of peace. While you may say it has never existed, I beg to differ. The culture of peace is evident in friendship, cultural exchanges, diplomacy and the United Nations. When we travel to other countries, isn't it ironic that we can't help but see more similarities than differences in people? Cultures and religions are different. Language is different, but when translated, we're all talking about the same things. Religions have different names for their gods, but they're still the same god.

It's also interesting that, while the world is in the throes of war, there has never been so much possibility for peace. The infrastructure is in place. Never before have we been so connected through Internet, commerce and travel in the world. For the first time in history, you could be carrying on a long-distance relationship with your girlfriend in Katmandu for free via the Internet and, if you really missed her, you could be transported to her doorstep in less than 24 hours for less than $1,000.

Where was your car made? Even if it is American, some of its parts were made in other countries. Your whole wardrobe, unless you made it yourself, came from somewhere else.

My point is this, we live in a global village where we are connected, like it or not. This culture of peace will require us to be aware that we are all sharing this tiny rock flying through space with everyone else. Why not get to know our neighbors? It's never been easier than now!

I have a challenge for you, if you choose to accept it. For the next month, try to see a piece of yourself in every person you meet. When you see that thing, even if you don't like it, accept it and respect it. Bless that person and their humanity—appreciate them.

That's good for a start. See how you feel. Banish your fear, talk to strangers. Make friends with immigrants. Try to view the world with a kindly eye. Then, once you have that down, go international! Take a trip to an exotic country! Hang out with the locals!

The key is to be open-hearted, and remember: United we stand, divided we fall.

 *Oliver Nims*

YOU NEVER NEED BE ALONE
Warren H. Wojnowski

Do you have fun living your life each day doing what you love? If not, what's holding you back? Are you feeling stuck because you're afraid or because you're unsure about how to go about it? Do you doubt your ability to actually do it, or do you worry other people will laugh at you for trying? Perhaps you feel alone.

Wouldn't it be terrific to wake up in the morning full of gratitude for the opportunity to live a great life today, and then to go out and live it on your own terms? How would that make you feel? What would that look like for you? You can experience all of that; you can begin to have it right now and you don't have to do it all alone.

I used to harbor many of these same fears and found myself living life as I was "supposed to," rather than how I wanted. I believed these two points were mutually exclusive. In fact, I spent 23 years of my adult life (not to mention most of my formative childhood years) believing that I had to live my life according to someone else's rules. I was locked into a formula that was essentially prescribed to me by the environment (parents, schools, government, church, etc.) in which I was raised. It went something like this: Get a good education, get a good job, work hard and keep your nose to the grindstone. Scrimp and save money, put off what you'd love to do until later, avoid taking any risks and, if you're lucky, you'll get to enjoy yourself in your twilight years. I felt completely alone, powerless to change my circumstances.

Does any of this sound vaguely familiar? In my particular case, it was actually working out reasonably well. I had a good job, was earning a reasonable salary and had achieved a degree of success in my life—or at least that's how it appeared on the outside.

On the inside, I was miserable. I was caught up in the struggle of my day-to-day life—choosing to make it a struggle without ever realizing what I was doing. I was in a sleepwalk of day-to-day drudgery. I was definitely not living the life of my dreams—the life I love.

Then one day, a whole new world of opportunity made itself known to me. I attended a conference based on the teachings of Robert Kiyosaki, author of *Rich Dad, Poor Dad*. It wasn't the information at the conference that was so amazing—although it was very helpful—rather, it was the environment. All of a sudden I found myself in a room full of like-minded people who not only wanted many of the same things I did, but many of them were willing to assist, encourage and even partner with me to follow my dreams.

I was no longer alone—I found I could choose to be part of a team. Since that time, I've discovered that there is an abundance of ways to tap into the power and energy of a team of like-minded people, and by doing so, I am instantly cured of any shortage of ideas, encouragement or feedback required to enable me to move forward.

I've learned that, while one plus one may equal two, one and one makes 11! By masterminding and working with others, there is an exponential increase in what you can achieve. You are suddenly able to tap into a virtually limitless range of ideas, concepts and information that can catapult you forward at a pace far beyond what you previously imagined possible.

In his book *Magic Ladder to Success*, Napoleon Hill cites the "Master Mind" as a fundamental principle of success because of the "mental chemistry" created when you have two or more individual minds harmoniously focused on a strong common desire. In other words, by deliberately seeking out other like-minded, passionate people who are as intently focused on the same dreams, you create a powerful team.

For me, the effect has been magical. Just by opening myself up to

masterminding with others and realizing I needn't do it alone, a thou-
sand-pound weight has been lifted from my shoulders and an unlimited
number of ideas and opportunities have come my way. I've completely
changed my circumstances, my life and who I am. I chose to leave my
corporate job behind and pursue my dreams.

I had no idea how any of it was going to work and how we'd be able to
pay the bills or keep the kids fed and clothed, but I believed in myself.
Looking back now, I suppose I just knew it would all work out—after
all, I no longer had to do things by myself.

Things have worked out beautifully. The sky didn't fall and the world
didn't end. Things have certainly changed, of course. We don't hang out
with all of the same people we used to. Our activities have become more
focused on family and friends, as opposed to scheduling things around
my job. We live a much more relaxed life, and we are active participants
in a genuine team—several teams, in fact.

It's all because of the tremendous sense of empowerment, ideas, feedback, encouragement and support we receive each day from our many
teams. By becoming actively engaged members of a magical team, we've
discovered a tremendous sense of community. We have a team that
expects us to live to our full potential, that supports and encourages us
when we lose sight of our path, that calls us on our actions when we fall
out of integrity, that inspires new ideas and goals and that ensures we
continue to learn and grow. We are unstoppable.

So what about you? What do you love? What are the things you'd love
to do right now with your life? Can you feel them calling you? If you
can, then listen and follow them. Follow them fearlessly, for you never
need be alone. Find others who will assist you in creating an environment in which you can succeed. There is no shortage of such people out
there if you really look.

Become part of a mastermind team and unleash your tremendous potential. Follow your dream by discovering the power of an intensely focused team, and soon you, too, will become unstoppable.

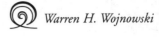 *Warren H. Wojnowski*

HOW MY TEENAGE SON WOKE ME UP
Diana Sterling

My teen years were agonizing. Do you remember the driving need to belong, to find a sense of who you were, to find some form of approval and acceptance from others? We admired—or resented—kids who showed some measure of confidence and success, and said, "How can I be like them?" We craved these things to fill an underlying need we all share: the need to find a sense of our own selves. I remember seeking my self and having a hard time at it, getting little support or encouragement from those around me. New insecurities, fears, struggles, pain, loneliness. But somehow I survived and went on to lead an adult life of more struggle, pain and difficulties. I had created more of it all.

At 39, I went through a transition. I put away my career as a film and video producer, and in one courageous move, jumped into professional life coaching, believing it would not only help others grow, but change me, as well. I had no idea what would really happen.

At the same time, my son and his friends were entering their preteens. Suddenly, new behaviors appeared, like grunting, hunching over and alternately ignoring me or responding in one-syllable sentences—you know the routine. Distance prevailed, grades plummeted and he was getting into bad situations. I would say to them, "Oh, I see you're practicing for your teenage years!" or, "Great grunt—you will really need that as you become a teen." I thought this was humorous. Whatever works, right? No "guide to teens" in sight.

But one life-altering day, my son asked me why I made such derogatory remarks about teenagers, and why every time he did something I didn't approve of, I'd say it must be a teenager thing. "You are like all the other adults I know—critical and hard on teenagers," he said. "Don't you think that makes me feel bad when you say things like that? Teenagers aren't broken, you know."

I froze. I had just been busted as a parent. In that one defining moment, I saw that, indeed, I had been making presumptions about what was true for all teens. I also realized that my son saw through to the heart of the matter. Why did I hold on to the casual notion that being a teenager was synonymous with being bad? Was I just going along with the pack—the media, other parents, the headlines?

I decided to hold my tongue while I sorted out my next step. I was uncharacteristically silent for about two weeks. Then, one day when he came home from school, the next defining moment occurred. As he came in the door, threw down his backpack and galloped into the house, I called out, "Hail, fine young son!" He looked at me as if I was from the moon. Aren't all parents? I caught my breath, thinking, "Oh dear, what have I done?" After an awkward silence in which we both stood wondering what to do next, he made the first move.

Jordan picked up his pack and walked past me, looking at me strangely. Then, in the moment it took him to walk from the front door to the kitchen, I saw him stand up a little straighter and lift his hunched head a bit higher. He turned to me and actually spoke in sentences. The ice was broken. I thought to myself, "Gee—that worked." I guess I am also the fine young mother. Maybe I could do more of this, if I dared.

I came to understand that this young person was asking me, the adult, for the opposite of what I was doing. My son was asking me to see him and his peers as positive, creative, searching, developing, wonderful individuals, not as a band of aliens from outerspace. He didn't want to be prejudged or disregarded, he wanted to feel respected and heard. He didn't want me to be ambivalent or remote. He wanted me to be a positive force for him, and consistently there for him during this time of inner and outer change.

Could I meet his natural need for separation without counter-withdrawal? Was there a way to still nurture and guide him without becoming anxious and oppressive? I contemplated how to guide this young man through conscious, positive attitude and loving support, rather than just holding my breath and hoping for the best for the next six to seven years. Was there some way I could learn what would help him to grow in the coming years, to lessen the loneliness and confusion that I had felt at his age? I came to realize that by applying my newfound professional coaching skills to parenting, I could do much to diminish my son's sense of isolation during the "searching" years. I could re-examine and reprogram my own thoughts and actions about teens.

I began to experiment with a different approach by interacting with my son in a way that honored him for exactly who and where he was at that point in time. I looked past his behaviors and respected the qualities he had been born with. After all, I decided, 14 is tough enough without your parents chiming in about what's wrong with you and what's wrong with teenagers in general all the time. I started using new vocabulary and stopped rolling my eyes at his "antics." I began to see him differently, complete and whole in all of his complexities and insecurities. I began to treat him differently as I adjusted something in myself. I became his life-coach—his parent as coach. Supporting, not rescuing. Nurturing, not destroying. Not parent as dictator, not parent as best friend. Parent as coach.

As his coach, *I* could be the one to rework our connection, and *I* could help him to develop the confidence he needed to move out into the world on his own. The real way forward came through him and hundreds of other young people I have spoken with who have expressed seven desperate requests of all of us:

If you **Respect** me,
I will hear you.
If you **Listen** to me,
I will feel understood.
If you **Understand** me,

I will feel appreciated.
If you **Appreciate** me,
I will know your support.
If you **Support** me as I try new things,
I will become responsible.
When I am **Responsible**,
I will grow to be independent.
In my **Independence**,
I will respect you and love you all of my life.

Thank you,
Your Teenager

During the teen years, my son and I didn't just survive—we thrived. Now, at 23, he is a capable, responsible and compassionate young man. I have found a way to respect, listen to understand, appreciate, support, build responsibility and foster independence. Join me in advocacy for every teen, every young adult and every child. The next time you see a teen, give an acknowledgement for who they are at the core of their being. We can influence a generation. My son now says to me, "Keep up the good work, Mom."

Thanks, Jordan, for waking me up. I couldn't have done it without you.

 *Diana Sterling*

A Garden of Eden
Dr. Sondra Batson-Braggs

One night while watching a televised ministry with my son Ondry, a force comes out of the television and knocks us both backward on the bed. He looks at me as if to ask, "Mom what's happening?" But then we smile and hug. The force takes over making us a bit weak, but soon lightens its grip. Ondry climbs down and leaves the room and I assume he wants to play with his toys or something. In any case, I can tell he doesn't want to stay around for "round two."

After Ondry's exit, I sit in my recliner, surrounding myself with spiritual wonder. Closing my eyes, I begin meditating to clear my mind and calm my total being. Soon I reach a level of communication with the universe that engulfs me in a magnanimous mass of energy. Vibrating from the top of my head to the tips of my toes, I know I'm where I am supposed to be and I am happy.

My body grows heavier as the moments pass. I try first to lift my feet and then my arms, but I am unable. So I decide to calmly sit, go with the flow and let the spirit take me where it wishes.

I am now levitating in mid-air, my feet no longer touching the ground. I'm drawn into a mist as I prepare for what is yet to come. My weighted eyelids are a struggle, but what begins to unfold in the darkness is a million times better than natural sight.

A "Garden of Eden" begins to appear. Wow, such beauty! To be in a place with unlimited love and goodness is awesome. I walk through a bright, deep green, meadow of luscious, soft grass, taking in its unfamiliar color. That's all I can see for miles and it is breathtaking.

Large trees emerge, thick with branches and bountiful foliage. They're so inviting, saying, "Come, Sondra! Take a rest and relax in our blessed shade and feel the wonderful, cool spring breezes."

I lie in the soft grass, rolling from side to side letting it surround me like covers over my body. My heart fills with so much joy and love that I sit up, lean against the trunk of the tree, twirling the grass between my fingers and take in even more of this awesome sight.

Something catches my eye. Just within an arm's reach is a single red flower. A bright, luscious red, so rich and vibrant, so full of life it almost hypnotizes me. It has a deepness that beckons, "Enter my domain and enjoy the eternal bliss." The fragrance is intoxicating. No word can describe this vision of loveliness. It's simply amazing!

Now I can hear the sound of a gentle waterfall a distance away. Turning to look, I am blown away to find that it's right beside me, appearing miraculously.

The crystal water looks like pure glass. Nothing can match its clarity and flawless visibility. Scooping some with my hands, I can imagine how it might feel to scoop wet air. It's so light that each droplet that falls makes a different musical note as it reunites with the brook from whence it came—like soft chimes, lulling me to a serene place of blissfulness.

In a soft whisper I hear, "Look over your left shoulder."

First, I see a bright, white light in the form of a ball, hovering in the distance. It begins to pulsate and then radiate beams of light from its core. A subtle outline of a man's head and upper torso emerges in the middle of this wonderful, bright beam. The light stretches its arms out and wraps around me in total divine love, and I hold on for dear life and begin to cry.

Suddenly a deep ominous voice murmers, "Yes Sondra, I really do love you! You've been a good servant, and I'm pleased with your works!"

The crying continues because I feel I'm home, around familiar surroundings with no interest in returning to my physical plane. I'm finally with someone who truly cares, and I don't want to give that up just yet.

"I will expand your consciousness to allow you to accept my love and see the whole situation from a higher viewpoint. Sondra, if your heart is pure (and only I can be the judge of that), the universe will bring truth into your life. It comes to different people in different ways. It may be through a book you read, a television show, a person you meet by chance or maybe even a doctor.

"While you may feel unimportant on this earth, you actually matter in the big picture of the universe and in how much you are truly loved. You see, you are a piece to the giant puzzle of my creative plan. The direction in which I am taking you involves working together with many others of like-mind to bring love and joy to our planet.

"Your purpose is to teach people to expand their lives through unwavering faith—the kind of faith that is unlimited. It's one that goes beyond the physical things that you can 'see' and makes what is 'impossible' become possible. By doing so, blessings will come. Favor, dreams and visions will come. Everlasting life and joy will come as they let go of their faith and see what the universe has in store for them.

"This cannot be done alone. It will take a multitude to accomplish such a task. If you stay focused, your path will cross with others at the right time, in the right place, and you will recognize them by the inner peace you experience while in their presence. Their works, along with yours, will correlate to form a cohesive whole for the greater good."

Looking up at him, I reply, "It's so peaceful and serene here! May I please stay with you now? Your love is so pure, my emotions so strong I don't want to leave. Please let me stay!"

He says again, in that commanding voice, "No. You have to go back. You must keep with the resolve to make a difference and to bring a new level of clarity and compassion to the planet. Your work is not yet done."

With a mighty force, he draws me back into my earthly body. Upon re-entry, I slowly drift into my recliner. My body is still heavy but that soon dissipates, and once flow fully returns, I am again mobile.

It takes a little time for my eyes to open fully. However, that gives me the opportunity to again reminisce on my wonderful experiences while this rebirthing process is taking place.

Rising from my chair to get my bearings, I can sense my body is some-how quite different. I proceed toward the bathroom and notice I am no longer walking. It's more like gliding or floating just slightly above the floor. My hair is standing on end and I imagine this must be, in some way, how Moses must have felt when he came down from Mt. Sinai.

I hesitate to look into the mirror for fear I will see rows of grey streaks running through my hair. Outwardly, I look about the same. The changes taking place are on the inside—my soul, my spirit. So much energy vibrating throughout my body.

This experience is a vivid and conscious travel of my soul. I immediately know this because, even though I can see every part with my mind's eye, I'm struggling for words to describe my adventure. What I see so clearly in my mind gets blocked coming through the channels of human expla-nation.

My language inadequately describes what lies ahead on this journey toward the heart of the universe, but I know we are all heroes of that voyage—a team. Along the way there are many trials and tribulations, tests and lessons that we must experience to perfect ourselves. We must work together. This journey of consciousness is not an easy one, but it is, by far, the most important and rewarding we'll ever take. If we don't doubt in our hearts, but believe the things we say will come to pass, we shall have whatsoever we ask in Jesus' name.

 *Dr. Sondra Batson-Braggs*

A NEW BEGINNING
Gary M. Anzalone

Most of us don't reflect on our lives until we face a major milestone. Significant events such as a graduation, marriage, divorce, the birth of a child or death of a loved one, career change, relocation or retirement may drive us toward self-evaluation. These events will cause us to think about what we have accomplished in our lives or in what direction we are heading. Well, one of these events was about to happen to me, but I was not aware of the powerful impact it would have. It was totally unexpected, and the feeling I had was so strong that I will forever remember it as a life-changing milestone.

It all happened two years ago when I was taking my son off to college. In the weeks before the move, we had made most of the arrangements, so only some small details remained. It was at that point when a heavy feeling began to take hold of me; it started building as the date neared. I was depressed and could not shake it.

Why was I feeling so debilitated? I had lost my energy—I could not motivate myself to do more than the minimum to get through the day. Could it have been due to self-reflection? The big picture is that my son was going off to college—an entirely positive milestone—yet it left me feeling somehow closed in. Despite that, I felt that a major phase in my life was complete, even though it had been years since my son or daughter had come running into my arms to greet me when I got home. Now my son would no longer be home, and when he came back, it would be only for a visit. Our little team was separating. The last few weeks leading up to the move out were a tremendous drain.

I have heard about the "empty nest" syndrome and have always thought my wife would be the one taking the brunt of the emotional upheaval. After all, she was the full-time mom who worked part-time—wouldn't she feel the sting of emptiness more than I? I was the full-time entrepreneur who had spent the past 20 years building a successful business. I worked long hours, but when I could allow myself to take time off, I worked even harder at enjoying time with my family. I also had several hobbies and sports activities to distract me.

Finally, the big day came; I had to hide my emotions. I did not want to darken the skies on the day my son was to take flight. We packed up the car and were still in the driveway when it hit me. It was the most amazing feeling, like jumping into cold water on a hot day. It was a feeling so strong that it took control of me. There was no time to think about it; I spoke immediately and said the following to my son:

"It's so amazing to see you in this stage of life; you have done so much and achieved so many things. I'm very proud of you. Yet, for all that you have accomplished, for all that you have seen and done, you are this day just beginning to start your life. It's a truly wonderful time and I'm so glad to be a part of it. There is a long road ahead of you with much to learn and experience. You have a future ahead that is limitless, full of opportunities and new experiences. The craziest thing about what I'm telling you is that I have just now suddenly realized that I have this very same feeling about myself!"

Whatever I had accomplished in my life thus far seemed dwarfed by my potential to do so much more with my future. I had never had this feeling before, not even when I was his age. At that age, all I remembered was insecurity and doubt as to what to do with the rest of my life. What road should I choose? How would I find my way? How would I make a living?

The temporary sadness I experienced resulted in an amazing self-awareness and new focus. I now began to rethink my future in a way that had never occurred to me. I was excited for my son's journey to conquer the world; it had given me the same ability to go out and make a difference in myself. I realized that my son leaving for school was as much about me as was it was about him, and what had started out as an emotional challenge was nothing short of an epiphany.

Now I have come full circle. Armed with motivation, focus and persistence, I can accomplish whatever I put my mind to. This rethinking of my future is an absolute gift. I had become too comfortable. Working through personal pain brought me to a higher level. Being too comfortable is limiting—it keeps you from growing to your potential and it can make you lazy.

In the two years that my son has been in college, I have realized more of my potential and achieved a higher quality of life. My wife and I have taken dance lessons and began riding a tandem bike. I have learned how to play the guitar and started a swimming fitness program. I have been active in fundraisers for some fantastic causes. Our last family vacation was a cruise to Spain, Italy, France, Greece and Turkey. I'm doing all the things I never found time to do before or that I thought I would do later in life upon retiring.

I fully believe what I told my son about his wonderful future. There is much to do—I promise myself that I will not be a bystander, I will enjoy my family and friends, learn something and improve myself every day. I will live life to the fullest every day, and I am ever thankful for the day that made it all happen, as I left my son standing on the crest of his new life.

Will you do something today that will make a difference in your life? Follow these three action steps to get you started. They are as easy as ABC:

> Appreciate what you have—family, friends and accomplishments. Think of something positive to put yourself in a good frame of mind. People gravitate toward those who have a smile on their faces, and you need them as much as they need you. Don't get caught up in being a complainer.

Be inspired and take your future into your own hands. Don't allow yourself to become too comfortable; form a plan and take action.

Commit to change and personal growth. Circumstances will change with time, so embrace the changes and grow. At times you may lose sight of what is truly important and you might be scared or tired, but stay committed to your greater future.

I am very fortunate to have had an experience that has allowed me to "wake up" and find a balance with work and life. I now avoid watching too much television and spending excessive amounts of time with e-mail. These things steal your time and give little back. Do more, be more, live more.

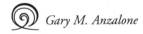 *Gary M. Anzalone*

LIVE THE LIFE YOU LOVE, PERSIAN STYLE
Thom Quinn

After spending a few minutes haggling in both English and Farsi, the merchant and I arrived at a fair price for a beautiful Persian carpet; I purchased it immediately. I had spent most of that June morning in 2004 visiting the wide variety of shops within the central bazaar of Shiraz, the garden city of Iran. It was lunch time, so I stopped at the teahouse next to the Bazaar Mosque for saffron rice and trout. As I inspected my newly acquired rug and enjoyed my meal, I reflected on how I had created my first dreams list just 10 years prior. It included a large number of interesting projects, such as visiting the ancient ruins of Persepolis and viewing the next Transit of Venus. When I compiled that original list, I never imagined that such diverse goals would have intersected; yet I was just hours away from fulfilling both of them. The two-fold purpose for my extraordinary journey to Iran was to explore the palace complex and UNESCO World Heritage site, Persepolis, and to witness a rare celestial event, the Transit of Venus (the first such occurrence of this astronomical phenomenon in 122 years).

As a busy professional, this 19-day adventure was my first prolonged sabbatical away from the office since entering the workforce. While sipping tea, I pulled out my leather-bound journal and jotted down a few ideas I had been considering all morning. Although I had several important awakenings—intellectual, spiritual and psychological—during my travels in Persia, it was during this relaxing lunch that I considered some precepts on living the life I really wanted. Although I had been thinking about these ideas for some time, it seems my wonderful day in Shiraz served as a mental catalyst, as my pen flowed for several hours. No, my Persian rug has not transformed into a flying carpet, but I do hope that the insights I had that afternoon are useful to you in achieving new heights and planning the life you truly desire.

The Life Triangle Test
Imagine an equilateral triangle, one where all three sides are the same

length and all three angles are an identical 60 degrees. The first angle represents Passions (P). The second angle is Strengths (S). The third angle is for Values (V). This is the ideal life triangle:

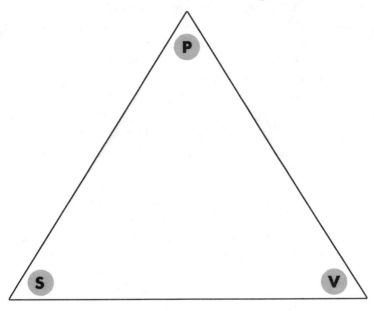

Think about your own life in terms of these three attributes:

Passions

The poet Rumi wrote, "Let the beauty we love be what we do." Likewise, the saying, "Everyone has been made for some particular work, and the desire for that work has been put in every heart," has been attributed to Rumi. Echoing these ideas, the great 20th century mythologist Joseph Campbell advised, "Follow your bliss," to his students and to not be afraid to live a life full of what you love. The definition of passion is literal: to be so excited that you cannot wait to wake up in the morning to work more on your endeavors. It should not be a surprise to anyone that when one is engrossed in an activity that is very enjoyable, one is likely to dedicate a high-quality effort for a longer period of time. So what do you love? Create a detailed list of your passions.

Strengths

This category combines both abilities and skills. Everyone has certain natural gifts and core competencies. One can excel in these areas after honing abilities with dedicated practice. After mastering certain skills, a person can produce superior results very easily. Experts can do extremely difficult things in a very short time frame. What are your innate abilities? What are your crucial skills? Create a detailed list of your strengths.

Values

Personal values are like the rudder of a ship, as they provide direction for your life. Values impart a particular worldview and provide you with a consistent framework and ethical principles to make choices. Decisions are easier when values are the guide. What is most important to you? What are your core beliefs? Create a detailed list of your values. What would your life triangle look like? Is something out of balance between your idealized life and reality? Most people have a life triangle that is lopsided, as one or more of the angles are out of alignment. When passions, strengths and values are congruent, you are truly living an optimal life, one that is overflowing with meaning and joy. Seek relationships and vocations that enhance the expression of all three at their highest level.

Productivity 101

Life is too short to be too serious or too foolish. The outer limit of a human life is approximately 43,800 days—and this number assumes a lifespan of 120 years, a feat of longevity few achieve. Do not be idle; do not wait for tomorrow. Time really is of the essence! You should embrace "do it now" as your daily mantra. It is vitally important that you become as productive as you can possibly be.

What is productivity? In the dictionary, it appears this noun is merely synonymous with the words "output" and "yield;" however, this is not an adequate explanation. I believe there is a straightforward way to look at the meaning that highlights how to be productive as well.

One aspect of productivity is effectiveness. Effectiveness relates to a person's individual or organizational mission, goals and projects. You can only be effective if you are focused on those important items that have a high pay-off, as these tasks are the ones that will bring you closer to your targets. Effectiveness means working on anything you truly desire; it is achievement-centric. Goal, project and task selection are all critical components of productivity.

The other aspect of productivity is efficiency. Efficiency means being able to pursue personal or organizational missions, goals and projects without wasted time, extra steps and increased costs. Efficient action needs to be both fast and competent. Rapid work is great and often important, but it is worthless if the quality is sub par. The most efficient tasks are those completed in a manner in which speed and excellence are both optimized. As a result, the methodology chosen for any task is a key factor for productivity.

My simple definition is as follows: Productivity is working on the right things in the best way.

Going beyond this uncomplicated definition, there is a very elegant equation for productivity: $P = E1 \times E2$, where:

P = Productivity
$E1$ = Effectiveness
$E2$ = Efficiency

Notice that the formula is not $P = E1 + E2$. In other words, productivity is not a summation of these two properties. Productivity is the product of effectiveness and efficiency.

Reflect again on the productivity equation above. You can be extremely effective without being efficient. Likewise, you can be very efficient without being effective, but remember: When you multiply a number by zero, you get zero. You cannot sacrifice one key attribute for the other and still be productive. This also suggests that small, incremental, positive adjustments to both effectiveness and efficiency on a daily basis can have dramatic results on your overall productivity.

Teamwork

While pouring my last cup of tea, the waiter shared a Persian saying with me: "Drops that gather one by one finally become a sea." I paused to consider how small increments (e.g. money, labor) compound and eventually produce a big result, just as a team pools together the individual time, talents and treasures of its members to create a sea of value. It is an easy concept: Two or more people with the same values, when working together toward a common goal, can easily accomplish more than one can alone, as their combined passions and strengths act as multipliers for the above productivity equation. A team can pursue a diverse set of tasks simultaneously while increasing both the quality and quantity of total output. Personal and organizational productivity and balance are critical to realizing the power of the individual as well as any team.

Regardless of what you do, it is vital that you live the life you love. In closing, I leave you with the wisdom of my favorite Persian proverb: "Go and wake up your luck!"

 *Thom Quinn*

OVERCOMING BIOLOGICAL BARRIERS TO TEAM POWER: WAKE UP YOUR CAPACITY
David N. Bailey, D.C., M.P.H.

Team power carries with it the implicit assumption that you, as a member or leader of a team, have the capacity to do what it takes. However, to engage in a collaboration requires intellectual and emotional capacity. Some folks have it, while others can find teamwork difficult, even with the help of effective team members. All that cheering, all those role-playing games and all those trust-building activities may not resonate with them.

Positive thinking can do the job—except in those cases where it doesn't. Just ask anyone who has struggled with being overweight for 30 years. No doubt, they've tried using the power of positive thinking, creative visualization and intense intention. They will tell you that there is more to it than that. They found themselves swimming upstream against the crushing current of their own chaotic biology.

The Four Fs of Failure
There are bonafide biological barriers to the bliss of successful team power. Fatigue, fear, mental fog and fixation (lack of creativity) drain the power from life. The encouraging news is that these four barriers can be overcome, but not without first recognizing them and creating effective strategies for tearing them down.

You Can't Brainstorm if Your Brain is Already Storming
The human brain is the most complex thing in the known universe. Your brain controls everything you feel, think and do. The quality and depth of your intellectual capacity and your emotional intelligence depend on how your brain works.

Your brain is actually not just one brain, but three, each stacked on top of the other. Your lowest brain, your *lizard* brain, controls the basic body functions of temperature regulation, digestion, heart rate and such. The lizard brain doesn't "think;" it instinctively reacts to signals from inside and outside the body.

On top of the lizard brain is the *mammal* brain, which governs—in a more sophisticated way—your endocrine system, mood, memory and emotional states. The mammal brain makes complicated and instantaneous decisions about threats and rewards, integrating the past with what is happening to you now.

The *human* part of the brain is a quarter-inch thick layer at the very top—more scientifically known as the *neocortex*. Its job is to regulate the animals below it. To do that, the neocortex must be flexible; nimble enough to exercise its supervision and control. Otherwise, the deeper animal brains go wild. The neocortex has a vast, interlinking network of neurons (nerve cells) that connects it to all parts of the brain and the body.

Another extremely powerful and virtually instantaneous communication system involves brain waves. Brain waves have the power to transmit and store vast amounts of information. Modern science is just beginning to scratch the surface of understanding how to use the power of brain waves. But we do know that changing brain wave patterns can work magic.

The brain can spend its time in a high capacity, flexible state, or find itself stuck in a rut of diminished power. Fear, mental fog and mental fixation—barriers to teamwork and blissful living—all come from these inflexible ruts.

For thousands of generations, human beings have worked hard to get out of their negative brain wave channels. Meditation, chanting, beating on drums, gongs or resonating bowls, dancing around fires, singing hymns and listening to music are all well-known methods to awaken the brain to a higher level of awareness. These work, but can be inefficient. Imagine what you could do if you were able to find and fix the ruts. Today, that can be done. There are sophisticated techniques used to "exercise" the brain out of fear, fog or low creativity that sap the power away from successful living.

Let me tell you about two highly effective therapies: Low Energy Neurofeedback (or LENS) which uses tiny radio wave impulses to unlock the brain, and what I call Good Vibrations Therapy. Good Vibrations Therapy, or neuroacoustics, is based on the science of using sound, light and vibration to change the pattern of brain waves. Each of these methods, in different ways, helps the brain to become more flexible and better able to escape from its negative grooves.

Creativity on Purpose: Modern Awakenings
We have moved from the Industrial Age to the Information Age, and now to the Age of Creativity. Creative and critical thinking skills are the currency of the modern workplace, and are vital to the team process. Creativity occurs normally in unexpected ways and at unexpected times. It just happens in those "A-ha!" moments when new ideas just pop into our heads out of nowhere.

However, creativity does not have to wait for serendipity to strike. With LENS and Good Vibrations Therapy, a properly trained doctor or therapist can find the barriers, and then engage specific protocols that can facilitate your brain to move into creative states with deliberate ease.

Fatigue Kills Team Power
Fatigue is a result of prolonged stress. When we are under protracted challenges or threats—or even if we just think we are—our body's ability to make energy is damaged. Stress weakens our adrenal glands, the main source of our energy production.

Think of the adrenal glands as heavy duty diesel engines. These engines help us pull the loads of work and family. However, just like any diesel engine, they can be overloaded and under-maintained. Your entire endocrine system—the glands that control your blood sugar and digestion, as well as your sexual energy and vitality—suffers when you drive yourself into adrenal exhaustion. The good news is that this is a correctable condition.

Many otherwise highly functioning individuals are just exhausted. If this description fits you, you probably would benefit from a functional endocrinology assessment for dysfunction in your endocrine system, especially your adrenal, thyroid and sex hormones. These tests provide a road map for natural therapy to awaken the innate power of your body to heal and re-regulate itself. With proper therapy, your energy and stamina returns in a matter of weeks. You have conquered fatigue.

After getting your endocrine system balanced you are ready to meet and exceed any challenge. Your joy returns; your relationships with family are more rewarding; you are more effective and efficient at your job and leisure activities. You are now an energized team member and team leader, because you now have your energy-producing capacity repaired and restored.

Wake Up the Power Within You
The four barriers to team power—fear, fatigue, fog and fixation—have a biological basis. You can tear down those walls through brain wave flexibility therapy and endocrine restoration and enhancement programs. Information on the Natural Waves Program is available at my Web site: naturalwavesprogram.com

Now your team works better, whether it be a team of many or a team of one.

 *David N. Bailey, D.C., M.P.H.*

Résumé vs. Attitude
Patrick Precourt

Eighty percent of your success is directly related to your attitude. The remaining 20 percent is dependent on your skills, systems and management capabilities.

You or your business is no better than the collective team that makes it up. So I ask you, why would you ever look for a new member for your team, an employee, associate or partner by first looking at résumé skills and management capabilities?

In 2003, I was working full time in a family business. I was married with two small children and was also working full-time to build a new company. The belief that I had to do it all myself left me in a situation where nothing was being done very well. I had to choose to change something, or it would change without me making a choice. I had to make some tough decisions. The first was to retire from my family business one of the toughest decisions I've had to make in business. Second, I had to admit I couldn't and shouldn't go it alone. Time to build a team!

Our team today consists of six in office (or home office) and around 15 or so associates.

The three keys I've found to building and attracting the right team members are critical to the team's success. They have little or nothing to do with a résumé.

1. The Winning Team Attitude
Attitude and the power of attitude have been written about by many authors, but I cannot overemphasize its importance. First, what is a winning team attitude? It is a belief that the success of the team comes before individual success; a belief that no one

individual is more valuable than the team, regardless of title; a belief that the team takes the credit for success and not an individual. These beliefs define their attitude. Second, the belief that quitting is not an option no matter how big the mountain to be moved; the belief that the only way to truly fail is to quit; the belief that the day-to-day failures are a required part of the process that leads ultimately to success. These beliefs define their attitude. Third, the belief that they do not need to be in the spotlight to perform; the belief that they must commit to being the absolute best in their roles; the belief that they cannot play the game at a level any greater than they practice, and therefore, they must practice as if they were playing in the Super Bowl. These three sets of beliefs make up the team attitude I'm looking for.

I had the opportunity to captain several rugby teams that have competed locally and internationally. Other than the military there is no environment, on or off the field, that so greatly relies on the cohesiveness of the team to be successful. The most valuable teammates I played with over my 12 years of competition all had this in common: team attitude. By maintaining the highest level of work ethic and commitment, despite whatever odds we were against, we would not lose—we could not lose—and this elevated everyone around them. An interesting point to be made: the players that rose as superstars ALL possessed team attitude, even though not all were superstars as measured by their overall skill.

2. Don't look for them, let them come to you.
This may seem a bit passive but indeed it is not. It's really a very purposeful attempt to attract the right people to our organization. How do we attract? Simple: give, and we will receive. We constantly seek to provide benefits to others, particularly in the professional environment. We look for players in the industry,

others that are out there doing it and not just talking about it. We then focus in on how we can help and benefit them. That's right: put out first! There are natural laws that simply take over from here–laws of attraction and reciprocation as well as others. A new teammate who has been attracted by this type of courtship and introduction will naturally be a provider of the same, and this is a fundamental characteristic of a team player. Give first, then you will receive attitude. It's an understanding that our success will be directly relative to the quality and quantity of service we provide. We want selfless players willing to give and to grow.

3. Focusing on strengths
We all have strengths; areas in which we excel and are passionate about. We also have weaknesses; areas where we really have to work hard just to be average. A strong passion fuels your team attitude, and passion feeds on the joy of achievement.

I have a few key strengths and many weaknesses, yet I have managed to reach a respectable level of success. Why? Because it doesn't matter that you have strengths and weaknesses; it matters that you know very clearly what they are! Your time needs be focused on working in your strengths.

Why? If you are working against your natural strengths the task will not come easy to you or, for that matter, will not be enjoyable. There will be no passion involved, and without the passion as a driving force, you will never be the best at what it is you have set out to accomplish. Why set out at all on a journey you can't possibly complete?

What does this have to do with building your team? Everything! The first person I ever hired (a professional hockey player who is now a business partner), was specifically plugged in to fill in many of my weaknesses. I understand that I'm outstanding at only a very few things. In order to have an outstanding, "the best there is" company, I had to surround myself with talent—not learned talent but natural talent—specifically in the areas where I was weak. This meant that I had to first appreciate my weaknesses and then be able to identify the strengths and weaknesses of others. Although this can be tough at times, a simple test is this: ask them what they LIKE to do. People tend to gravitate towards likeable tasks based on natural skill sets.

Résumés, referrals and job history all play a role in hiring–but not on our team. I can train you to be "over the top" successful, but I can't motivate you to do anything. Motivation, drive, purpose, attitude–team attitude–all come from within. Attitude drives actions, which drives results. Get the right attitudes on your team, place them in their natural strengths, and you just built a DREAM TEAM!

 *Patrick Precourt*

HE'S ON YOUR TEAM
John Baldwin

I was born on February 20, 1961, and am the oldest of three boys. My father worked as a computer programmer at Independent Life Insurance and my mother was a homemaker. We were a normal family living in a typical suburban neighborhood. However, it wasn't a fairy tale for me.

My strongest memory of childhood is that I was not good at anything I attempted. My little brother, Jay, was the shining star and the apple of our dad's eye. Dad didn't have much patience with my slow learning, especially since it always seemed to take a while for me to catch on to even the smallest concepts. I always wound up in tears over my homework, I wasn't good at sports and I had trouble making friends. So, I just followed my brothers around instead of living my own life.

I often stayed at home by myself and began reading. My mom signed us up for a book-of-the-month club, which allowed me to read books such as *Flicka, Black Beauty* and *Tom Sawyer*. These stories cleared my mind and gave me new hope of a fairy tale ending for my life.

Tired of seeing me sit around at home, my mother enrolled me in Boy Scouts at the age of 9. Shortly afterward, my grades started dropping. I went from making As and Bs to Cs and Ds. Now, I can look back at those grades and understand what happened. My scoutmaster, who had become a friend of the family, was sexually abusing me. I kept this horrible reality to myself until I finally broke down and told my mother when I was 34. Why did I wait? My mother and father always fought, which eventually led to divorce in 1969. I didn't want to bother them with my problems, and for some reason, I thought they already knew what was going on. Despite growing up in a religious home, I lived with shame and confusion for many years. I knew enough about the Word of God to know that this wasn't right, but my abuser was an adult and I was always taught to trust and obey adults. Besides, he was a friend of the family; I didn't think anyone would have believed me.

With this situation came many other problems. My self-esteem, individuality, confidence, sexuality, trust and social behaviors were all affected. When I was 16, my brother, Jeff, and I were allowed to go to a concert. We were stranded there and wound up being the last few waiting when the concert was over.

The only other people there were the "Bible thumpers." They overheard our conversation about our mother not being able to come get us and offered us a ride. I called my mom, and she insisted that we ride with them. They drove a Volkswagen and about eight people were shoved into it. When we were in the van, they paid no attention to us. They just did what they do: prayed and sang about Jesus. That evening, one of the girls gave me a Bible. I now know that was the beginning of a new life for me.

I was raised in a religious home and was taught about good and evil, but I also knew that Sunday was the worst day of the week for our family. That's when we fought and argued the most about trying to keep a schedule. But I thought I'd give it another try. I started reading the Bible and discovered that I liked what I read. I'm not saying that I had a mountaintop experience and everything was right as rain from then on, but I received a great amount of peace and assurance that my life was worth living.

This was a form of spiritual healing for me. I was introduced to what I now call the Way, the Truth and the Life—Jesus. Life wasn't made perfect magically, but I knew that I had a purpose. I still dealt with low self-esteem and confidence but now I had direction.

This new knowledge gave me what I needed to move forward. I served in the Army from 1981 to 1984. After I got out of the service, I had trouble keeping jobs, but I kept going. I wouldn't quit. At 33 years of age, I was working for $6 an hour, 20 to 30 hours a week, with no vehicle or money, living with my mother and my 16-year-old son. I figured out that I liked to do yard work, so I started a business to do what I enjoyed.

My story continues with more restarts and growth, but what I want you to know is that there is never a reason to stop moving forward. Life is great when you know how to live it and live *with* it. My relationship with a living Savior was the peace in my life that surpassed all understanding. He says that He will never leave nor forsake me. The poem "Footprints" says it best: "During your times of trial and suffering, when you see only one set of footprints, it was then that I carried you."

Remember, you are never alone.

 *John Baldwin*

UNITING GENIUS
Kimberly King

For the past 20 years, I've been a passionate student, teacher and practitioner of the principles of transformation and conscious evolution. I've participated in dozens of conferences, read numerous books and journals and become part of communities in prayerful pursuit of the highest good.

In 1997, I made a pilgrimage to Brussels on a quest to explore new paradigms in creative collaboration and enlightened leadership. I spent days in rapt conversation with colleagues across the continent, wondering what might be possible if we found more ways to work together.

One of our conveners was distinguished professor and author Warren Bennis, who had published a groundbreaking study he called Organizing Genius. The focus of his research was to analyze teams that had accomplished the extraordinary and to compare great groups in history whose efforts made a dent in the Universe.

The examples chosen were wide-ranging, from the young Walt Disney's pioneering innovations in the field of animation to the crew that created and marketed the Apple personal computer to the controversial Manhattan Project whose scientists produced the atomic bomb.

- The first clear observation to emerge was that genius is not exclusive to any one industry or discipline, nor is it the byproduct of an Ivy League education, economic privilege or a particular geography. The second observation was that genius can, indeed, be organized and used for destructive purposes or harnessed for public good.

- We learned that all great groups begin with a vision and a deeply compelling mission. Most consider the mission a mandate or a higher calling from God. Great groups always have an enemy—

something they are fighting. They view themselves as winning underdogs struggling against the odds to change history or fate.

- A great group is a collaboration of talented individuals with complimentary skill-sets. Each member is a proven professional and leader in his or her respective field. Great groups master the difficult art of working well together because they are driven by their passion to realize the collective dream.

- Great groups and great leaders are symbiotic; they organically create greatness in each other. It is the mission, rather than the leader, that sets the course and guides the way.

As I considered these correlations, I pondered what these principles meant to me and how they could be applied to anyone's ordinary life to create extraordinary results. What materialized was a simple but salient formula: The power of purpose + the power of focus + the power of teams = a transformation of the world.

In 2002, I was granted an opportunity to prove the truth of this equation. It gave me a unique chance to experience the vast potential of a focused and purpose-centered team.

Like all great groups, we converged around a common dream: in this case to make a difference for the cause of curable blindness throughout the world. Our mission was to bring hope and our purpose was to ameliorate suffering for more than 40 million people living with blindness around the globe.

Our enemies were time, lack of information, injustice and poverty. Our weapons were focus, creativity, intelligence and grace. We formed a team of committed individuals—most of us total strangers—and gave ourselves just 12 short hours to do something that had never been done.

Approximately half the team had some background in curable and preventable blindness, and the other half knew very little. This was part of the experiment and the metaphysical magic we were there to prove. We were definitely daring underdogs, rising to embrace a daunting endeavor. From a place of focused intention, we began our search for solutions.

To our delight, the audacious expedition proved successful. We shifted design specs and streamlined manufacturing for a key surgical instrument; by pooling our strengths we devised improvements in the overall delivery system, reducing costs, and improving efficiency by nearly a thousand percent. This represented a bona fide breakthrough that would eventually help restore sight to millions more who were blind.

It is impossible to convey the sense of pride we each felt to have accomplished our goal and the deep humility and joy we felt to have participated in this special experience. Though there was work yet to be done before we could present a tangible outcome, we all knew in our souls we had seeded a minor miracle that day. We started out as twelve strangers with seemingly little in common, and through the bond of sacred service we became a great group for one unforgettable day.

Some contributions were large, others were small but all were essential to the achievement. Each perspective was needed to create the lens through which we were able to see a new collective vision: a future of light for so many who were living in darkness.

This is only a glimpse of what is possible when an individual truly grasps how her contribution is not only important but also necessary. Each of us has a spark of genius within. When we focus our genius with passion, imagination and intention, we invite the universe to ignite the fires of transformation.

This is also a deep insight into that which can only happen when the community comes together and consciously unites each individual genius with the collective brilliance that is humanity.

If peace is to prevail on Earth, it will require both our individual and our collective efforts, and that shift can only begin with you and me.

My prayer is that all of us will stand up for a cause we passionately believe in and apply this sacred equation, creating circles of possibility that will transform our world.

 *Kimberly King*

YOU GOTTA WANTA
Lee Beard

I remember it well; I can see it today as vividly as the day it happened.

It was during a presentation from a small-town basketball coach. He told a story about one of his championship players. It is a story of desire, and the miraculous changes that desire can make in our lives.

When he first saw her, three ideas were trying to balance themselves in his mind. First, he saw the potential for her to be a star, although less experienced coaches might have missed the tell-tale signs of future brilliance. Second, he noticed that she was overweight and out-of-shape; she had no business in sports–especially a sport that required constant movement and endless exertion. Third, he reminded himself that his was a small school in a small town, and the choices were few.

The story of chance is amazing. What if he had continued to look for some "perfect" player? What if he had decided that it would take too much work to convert this potential player into the real thing?

But the most powerful thing that I remember from his story was the result of his constant instruction; the interaction of the coach (teacher) and the player (student). When she found it difficult to run the simplest of drills, he told her, "You gotta wanta get from one end of the court to the other." It was the same at every practice: "You gotta wanta, you gotta wanta, you gotta wanta." It soon became her battle cry as she practiced and then, as she played: "You Gotta Wanta!"

The kid who wouldn't have been picked to play became a champion.

This had such an impact on me that I made a sign which reads (you guessed it), "You gotta wanta," and placed it on my desk. Even now, it seems to say it all: "You gotta wanta."

For some reason, it sums up the essence of passion. A little dab will do, but a whole lot more won't hurt you, either. Can you tell that I've become attached to that phrase?

As I go through the day, I often recall the words and the story. It brings a smile to my heart and a renewed determination to my spirit. I am reminded that "I gotta wanta" complete the task—no matter how tedious or commonplace or difficult—to get to the end of the project. Without that spirit of "gotta wanta," every obstacle is insurmountable; every challenge is a defeat.

I would wish for you the discovery of a passion that stirs your spirit and energizes your life so that each day is fun and each task is exciting. I believe that would make life better, and would make you a better person in the eyes of each one you meet. I hope to stir up your "wanta" so that you "gotta" do it.

 Lee Beard

AUTHOR INDEX

Gary Anzalone was born and raised in Brooklyn. He lives with his wife and two children on Long Island. He graduated from New York University with a BS in Technology and Industrial Education. Gary is co-founder of a business that started in his parent's basement in Brooklyn. During his tenure, the company has grown from a two-person venture to a 70-man business. He is a valuable resource to fellow business owners, providing both his support and problem-solving skills. He enjoys bringing people together for networking and inspiring them to maximize their company's potential.

Address: 243 Dixon Ave.
Amityville, NY 11701
Telephone: 516-658-0856
E-mail: gma59@optonline.net

Dr. Bailey has earned degrees from Texas A&M University, Texas Chiropractic College and Texas A&M University Health Science Center School of Rural Public Health. His special interests are in executive health restoration and corporate creativity enhancement programs.

Address: 200 B East 24th St.
Bryan, TX 77803
Telephone: 979-822-2225
Web site: naturalwavesprogram.com
E-mail: drbailey@naturalwavesprogram.com

John Baldw[...] the Second Chance Man, is changing lives all over the world by empowerin[...]g them a second chance.

Telephone: 904-259-4743
Web site: www.startyourmlmbusiness.com

Bill is the ultimate underdog/survivor/achiever overcoming personal circumstances and tragedy to rise to the top of corporate America. He and his wife, Kathy, travel the country, sharing their stories of how they created their successes and how they dealt with their challenges. It is their life's goal to do for "failure" what Betty Ford did for alcoholism and Susan Komen did for breast cancer.

Address: 8252 So. Harvard, Suite 150
Tulsa, OK 74137
Telephone: 918-388-3328
Web site: www.billbartmann.com
E-mail: bill@billbartmann.com

Sondra Batson-Braggs attended Oklahoma State University in Stillwater, Oklahoma, before receiving her Bachelor of Science degree from Central State University in Edmond, Oklahoma. She graduated from Palmer College of Chiropractic in Davenport, Iowa, and currently practices in northwest Oklahoma City.

> Batson-Braggs Chiropractic Center
> Address: 4220 NW 23rd St.
> Oklahoma City, OK 73107
> Telephone: 405-943-3025
> E-mail: healinghandssbb@aol.com

Larry is the connector of millionaires and billionaires–connecting others for the greater good, teaching others how to get whatever they want in a fraction of the time–guaranteed. He is the author of the upcoming book, *Connect and Grow Rich*. He is also the president of the Speakers and Authors Networking Group, and is the former chairman of the Tsunami Disaster Relief Project. His life's goal is to raise a billion dollars for worthy non-profits. You can learn more about him and download $700 in valuable resources.

> Website: http://www.larrybenet.com

Lee is a former television producer and business developer. He lives in Arkansas when not traveling as the co-creator of the *Wake Up Live the Life You Love* book series. Lee is an author featured in more than a dozen motivational and inspirational volumes. He concentrates on bringing the power of the Wake Up network to bear on the challenges of business development. If you've had a "wake up" moment you would like to share, visit wakeupmoment.com to tell your story!

> Web site: www.wakeupmoment.com
> E-mail: lee@wakeuplive.com

Brugger is a marketing and business growth consultant, a speaker and an author. He lives with his wife, Dianne, owner of Miss Dianne's Daycare. They have five grown children and have ten grandchildren.

> Address: 219 South Third Street, Coshocton, Oh 43812
> Telephone: (740) 623-8170
> Website: www.BruggerResources.com
> Email: Brug@BruggerResources.com

Roger "Phil" Gilliam is the proud father of Matthew, is a Certified Public Speaker/Trainer, President of AverageGuy, Inc., and has spent years in "real world" research on relationships and how men interact with women in all stages of the relationship. He has set a personal mission to directly change the lives of at least one million men as it pertains to their long-term relationships and happiness.

Web site: www.averageguyhelp.com
E-mail: phil@averageguyhelp.com

Debbie is an Internet marketing consultant, trainer, Web site portfolio manager and travel agent. Drawing from her successful sales and management experience in real estate, investing, travel, financial planning and the Internet, Debbie helps empower others to be successful in their own unique businesses. In her free time she enjoys adventure travel and swims not only with dolphins, but also with stingrays, manatees and sea turtles.

Telephone: 866-688-DEBB
Web site: DebbieGriffyn.com, DolphinSwimAdventures.com,
TravelProsNetwork.com, HomeBasedTravelAgentJobs.com
E-mail: DebbieGriffyn@yahoo.com

Design Your Life With Us is based on adding value to the community by assisting people in establishing a strong foundation of security and integrity. We are assisting people in developing a sense of peace and loyalty. We are encouraging people to build a team and tap into their own creativity. We are focused on creating the awareness of Personal Responsibility and financial freedom.

Life Designer Extraordinaire
Address: 960 85th Street
Amery, Wisconsin 54001
Telephone: 866-512-5406
E-mail: Jean@DesignYourLifeWithUs.com

Monica is a CEO and entrepreneur. She has preformed stand-up comedy for more than 12 years and is slowly building the foundation for her championship team for motivational and inspirational speaking.

Telephone: 403-290-0930
Web site: www.truemonica.com
E-mail: monica@truemonica.com

Bill King is an author, trainer, speaker and personal coach with more than 25 years of experience managing people. He has an extensive background in training and teaching others. In his business career, he has written manuals, training guides and step-by-step process guides. In December 2005, he decided to use these experiences to help others and began writing down ideas and concepts that he personally used to improve his life and find his life's purpose. He is the author of *7 Days to Inner Peace: The Building Blocks of Awareness* as well as *The Building Blocks of Creation: An Adolescent's Guide to Awareness.*

Web sites: www.posiTRACT.com/wakeup, www.idontstink.com
E-mail: wakeup@posiTRACT.com

Kimberly King is a visionary and global leader in the realms of cause-related marketing, public-private partnerships and business as an agent of world benefit. Kimberly is passionately engaged in women's empowerment, children's education and using the tools of technology and communication to heal and transform our world. Kimberly's commitment is to live a life in service of God that edifies compassion and peace.

The Peace Company
Telephone: 802-453-7191 or 262-642-7799
E-mail: Kimberly@thepeacecompany.com, Kimberly@SophiaCircles.org

Master coach and trainer, co-author of *Portable Coach.*

Telephone: 819-845-1115 fax: 819-845-5111
E-mail: Yulcoach1@axion.ca

A former college dropout, Dan "The Man" Lok transformed himself from a grocery bagger in a local supermarket to a multi-millionaire. Dan "The Man" Lok came to North America with little knowledge of English and few contacts. Today, Dan "The Man" Lok is one of the most sought-after business mentors on the Web, as well as a best-selling author. His reputation includes his title as the world's No. 1 Web site conversion expert.

Quick Turn Marketing International, Ltd.
Address: 141 - 6200 McKay Ave., Suite 964,
Burnaby, BC, Canada V5H 4M9
Web site: www.WebsiteConversionExpert.com
E-mail: info@websiteconversionexpert.com

Johnny Morney is an award-winning speaker and published author. He co-authored a book with some of the sharpest minds of our time such as Johnny Wimbrey, Bryan Flanagan and Jack Canfield titled *Multiple Streams Of Inspiration.* He also authored a life-transforming ebook titled *7 Phenomenal Razor Sharp Strategies to Finally Take Responsibility for Your Success or Else.* As a proud member of the Les Brown Speaker's Network and the John Di Lemme Millionaire Lifestyle Club, he is committed to working with people who struggle with addiction, destructive behavior or any other form of bondage that is holding them captive. Johnny wants you to know that you are just a step away from your personal and spiritual transformation in every area of your life. Find out how Johnny literally turned tragedy into triumph by visiting his Web site.

Web site: www.JustaStepAway.com

Salon owner and educator.

E-mail: wakeupbeauty@yahoo.com

Ph.D. Candidates in Entrepreneurship.

The Entrepreneur Doctors: "Tell us Where It Hurts"
Address: Las Vegas, NV
Telephone: 702-336-8709
Web site: www.EntrepreneurDoctors.com, www.SuccessMasteryEvents.com
E-mail: interact@entrepreneurdoctors.com

The author received a Ph.D. from Columbia University in Anthropology and Comparative Education. He has studied Ancient Egypt and has been a student of the Bible from "Word of Faith Camp" through Kenneth Hagin, Sr. He published *The Roots of Our Faith: Ancient Egypt and the Bible and Jesus Christ: The Missing Years & the Mysteries.* He lives with his wife in Yonkers, New York.

Telephone: 914-968-0111
E-mail: drocansey@yahoo.com

Dr. Vicki is a passionate child psychologist and parenting expert known worldwide for her practical, parent-friendly tips. Her mission is to help and support parents in raising happy, successful kids and enjoying the ride! She is the founder of the Better Parenting Institute™: Because the Better You Do The Better They Become!

Telephone: 321-722-9001
Web site: www.BetterParentingInstitute.com
E-mail: DrVicki@AskDrVicki.com

Mr. Precourt is a highly successful self-made entrepreneur, businessman, mentor, public speaker and educator. Patrick has taken his team mentality, cultured from years on the rugby pitch and adapted it to today's business world. He now trains fellow business owners nationwide in the same trench-proven team strategies that have lifted his company to an authority and leader position in the industry.

Telephone: 860-571-0568 Fax: 860-371-3869
Web site: nsehomes.com
E-mail: pat@nsehomes.com

Thom Quinn is a professional coach, productivity expert and creativity catalyst, as well as a trainer, speaker and author. Coach Thom assists individuals, teams and organizations in achieving their primary goals rapidly, effectively and efficiently. He consistently helps clients get twice the juice from half the fruit by utilizing the principles of positive psychology. He is also the founder and CPO (Chief Possibility Officer) of Possibility Coaching and Consulting, LLC. His new book, *The Little Purple Book of Productivity*, will be released in 2008.

Address: 2701 University Ave., Suite 2-472
Madison, WI 53719
Telephone: 608-442-0471
Web sites: www.thomquinn.com, www.possibilitycoaching.com, www.littlepurplebook.com
E-mail: thomquinn@possibilitycoaching.com

A No. 1 best-selling author, Gregory Scott Reid has become known for his energy and candor on the speaker's platform and his signature phrase "Always Good!" An experienced entrepreneur in his own right, he has become known as an effective leader, coach, and "The Millionaire Mentor."

Phone: 877-303-3304
Web site: www.AlwaysGood.com

The Anthony Robbins Foundation is a non-profit organization created to empower individuals and organizations to make a significant difference in the quality of life for people who are often forgotten—youth, homeless and hungry; prisoners, the elderly and disabled. Our international coalition of caring volunteers provides the vision, the inspiration, the finest resources and the specific strategies needed to empower these important members of our society.

Web site: www.anthonyrobbinsfoundation.org

Allan is always ambitious and wanting the good life. Introduced to network marketing, he discovered the reason most people fail—income depends on a team effort, which means motivating your team. Allan began to learn how and finally became more interested in motivation and personal development than network marketing.

Web site: www.roughseasafeharbour.com
E-mail: allan@roughseasafeharbour.com

CEO, New Generations International
Author, Trainer, Speaker
The Parent as Coach Approach: Seven Ways to Coach Your Teen in the Game of Life (White Oak Publishing, 2008), by Diana Sterling, ISBN # 0-9702255-2-0."

Telephone: 505-247-2902
Web site: www.dianasterling.com or www.parentascoach.com
E-mail: diana@dianasterling.com

Creator of *Wake Up...Live the Life You Love*. With more than 12 million stories in print, his message is reaching an international audience. Steven E has joined many of his co-authors at seminars and lectures. Some of these include Dr. Wayne Dyer, Deepak Chopra, Eddie Foy III, Donald Trump University, and many more inspirational souls.

Web site: www.wakeuplive.com

Dr. Trimble was born, raised and is doing quite well. A former art teacher, real estate broker and seminar speaker, he's been a chiropractor for more than 20 years and is the owner of the Health and Wellness Clinic—a chiropractic, physical therapy, massage and acupuncture clinic in Layton, Utah. He's also an all-around good guy.

Address: 1025 N. Main St.
Layton, UT 84041
Telephone: 801-544-4333
E-mail: healthwellness@relia.net

After spending 23 years in the financial services industry, during which he served as an executive with two of North America's largest financial institutions, Warren woke up and walked away from the corporate world. He now lives life on his own terms, operating a very successful home business with his wife Michelle. They spend their time traveling, having fun with their children, friends and family and teaching others to do the same.

MicWar Lifestyle Solutions
Address: 117 Perron St.
Lorette, MB, Canada, R0A 0Y0
Telephone: 204-878-4564
Web site: www.InspiredAbundance.com
E-mail: info@inspiredabundance.com

Co-Founders of JMG Incorporated
Jennifer, Matthew and Gayook have successfully established a working environment where
each other's strengths are supported and their weaknesses are transformed to create a stronger,
cohesive unit. JMG passes on their knowledge through leadership and performance programs.
They explore the roles established in families and their impact on leadership style, work ethic
and, subsequently, a company's overall sustainability to create a supportive, successful work environment. Along with their corporate programs, lectures and executive coaching, JMG offers parenting, family and individual programs.

E-mail: jmgpartner@aol.com

Glenn Wooten Sr. lives in St. Charles, Missouri, with his wife and four children. A full-time
employee of the U.S. Postal Service of 27 years, he has been inspired to achieve the impossible by
educating the public on the dangers of identity theft. Many times legal counsel is needed, in
addition to identity restoration services. Glenn is also committed to mentoring others to earn six
figures in the next five years.

Address: P.O. Box 344
Hazelwood, MO 63042
Telephone: 314-712-2387
Web site: www.millionairemindmotivation.com
www.glennwooten.com

Sharon is a passionate personal leadership coach and motivational speaker working with individuals and groups wanting to achieve a more balanced and fulfilling life. She is a visionary of
what people's potential can be and believes in the power of one. Her mission is to inspire and
encourage people to live their best lives with compassion, love and integrity. Her signature
keynote, "Live By Choice, Not By Chance," motivates individuals and organizations to gain clarity on ensuring the quality of their life or organization.

Web site: www.livewithintent.com
E-mail: Sharon@livewithintent.com

Debbie Wysocki is the owner of Women with Dreams and Residual Money Secrets, companies that empower the average person to live an extraordinary life by building a profitable business. She is a wife, mother, volunteer, speaker, syndicated columnist, author and investor. As a
former financial analyst, she learned the importance of financial independence and having time
to enjoy family and friends. Women with Dreams and Residual Money Secrets were created with
the big picture in mind—bringing like minds together as a way to help others live their dreams.
                                 Telephone: 954-781-6629 or 800-576-3767
              Web site: www.WomenWithDreams.com, www.ResidualMoneySecrets.com
                             E-mail: Debbie@WomenWithDreams.com

WAKE UP...
LIVE THE LIFE YOU LOVE

The Power
Of Team

RESOURCES

RESOURCES

John Di Lemme
Di Lemme Development Group, Inc.
Address: 931 Village Blvd., Suite 905 - 366
West Palm Beach, FL 33409-1939
Web site: www.FindYourWhy.com

John Di Lemme was a 24-year-old stutterer working in his family art gallery who dreamed of becoming a world-renowned motivational speaker. Desperate to achieve his goal, he answered an ad that allowed him to break free from the art gallery and build his own business. Through his business, John built a massive marketing team of over 25,000 representatives in 10 countries and earned a seven-figure, passive residual income. Seven years later, John retired to South Florida where he continues to live the life of the rich and not-so-famous.

John has achieved great success as an international motivational speaker, accomplished author and multi-million dollar entrepreneur. His latest best-selling books are *Find Your Why & Fly! – The Ultimate Success Factor* and *Champions are Born, Losers are Made*. John is also the co-host of an international television show and was a featured real estate investor on CNBC Power Lunch. John shocks millions globally by exposing the truth about how to achieve monumental life success despite the labels that society has placed on you. Through his award winning live seminars, power-packed training programs, live tele-classes, weekly ezine and website (www.FindYourWhy.com), John Di Lemme has made success a reality for thousands worldwide.

"You must be absolutely clear about your goal and be relentless in pursuit of your Why."—John Di Lemme

RESOURCES

Bill Bartmann
8252 So. Harvard, Suite 150
Tulsa, Oklahoma 74137
www.billbartmann.com

Bill is the ultimate underdog/survivor/achiever overcoming personal circumstances and tragedy to rise to the top of corporate America. Bill and his wife, Kathy, have individually graced the covers of national business magazines—Kathy on the cover of Forbes, and Bill on the cover of Inc. They were also listed individually in the Forbes 400 wealthiest people in America. One national magazine ranked them number 25.

What can Bill Bartmann do for you?

If you'd like to finally understand what is holding you back in life and in business, and to break through this barrier to achieve success, then keep reading.

Bill will show you the secret to accomplishing any goal without buying or selling real estate, trading stocks, or quitting your job (unless that is your particular goal). His seminar is the only one conducted by a person who has actually achieved billionaire status.

There are dozens of self-help and success seminars that focus on teaching you how to exploit opportunities in real estate, stocks and bonds and a whole list of other "get-rich" techniques. Bill's seminars are remarkably different. He doesn't teach people how to buy real estate, although he owns millions of dollars worth of real estate. He doesn't teach people how to buy stocks and bonds, although he has personally done over $3 billion in Wall Street transactions. Instead, he shows them how to be successful with the tools they already have.

Visit his Web site to see a list of venues where Bill will be speaking.

Noetic Pyramid

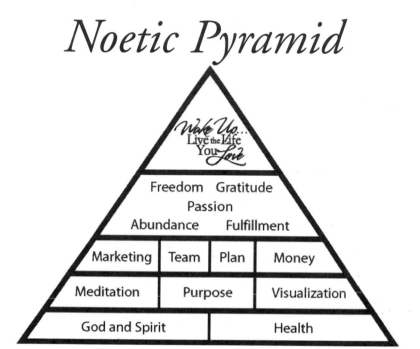

The Noetic (no-EH-tik) Pyramid is a systemic way of looking at the benefits of learning and implementing the attitudes, beliefs and behaviors that must always precede real abundance in life.

NOESIS (no-ë´-sis, noun) [Greek. To perceive] 1. Philosophical: Purely intellectual apprehension. 2. Psychological: Cognition, especially through direct and self-evident knowledge. Noetic (adjective)

There is a way to know; therefore, there is a way to know what to do in life. The answers are not concealed from us, but are available through noesis: a purely intellectual process which gives us sure answers, if only we will look and grasp what we see.

But no one can see—or even look with energy and purpose—unless the mind is clear and the attention is directed. We need a guiding principle that gives us a direction and a foundation.

Building on what they have discovered over years of working with teachers, mentors, motivators, philosophers, psychologists and business leaders, Steven E and Lee Beard have devised the Noetic Pyramid: a structure of beliefs and learning that takes us from the firmest of foundations to the kind of life we can most enjoy; the kind of life which can most benefit those around us; the kind of life that may change the world.

Foundations
With your firm faith in God, you have the proper perspective to process all instructions that you receive. Then, when you give adequate attention to your health, you have a solid foundation to allow you to learn and utilize what we call The 7 Secrets of Living the Life You Love.

Charting the Course
Then we must develop the internal structures of abundance: find your purpose through meditation or prayer, then visualize your desired future. To embark on this process without a firm grounding in belief and without the physical tools to support your mind and spirit, you are almost sure to be disappointed.

Reach Out to Expand the Possibilities
The Pyramid then leads you from a firm foundation to the external techniques of planning, teamwork, marketing and acquiring the necessary money. None of these external elements will be meaningful without the foundational elements, but neither will these essential elements inherently lead to abundance.

Abundance and Gratitude
We must realize the benefits of learning and utilize the internal structure and external techniques to create abundance, freedom, gratitude and fulfillment so we can truly live the life we love. An abundant life has meaning beyond ourselves, so we must seek to improve the lives of others. When we use our freedom to the benefit of others, when we are thankful for the opportunity to share the blessings of a materially abundant life, then we are fulfilled beyond our ability to imagine.

This is what we want everyone around the world to do: Wake Up...Live the Life You Love.

WAKE UP...
LIVE THE LIFE YOU LOVE

The Power
Of Team

A GIFT FOR YOU

A GIFT FOR YOU

Wake Up...Live the Life You Love wants to give you a gift that will get you moving on the path to personal abundance. Please visit www.wakeupgift.com today so you and your team can start on your way to the future you deserve!